Is Salami and Eggs Better Than Sex?

MEMOIRS OF A HAPPY EATER

Is Salami and Eggs Better Than Sex?

MEMOIRS OF A HAPPY EATER

by Alan King
and Mimi Sheraton

LITTLE, BROWN and COMPANY
BOSTON / TORONTO

FIRST EDITION

Library of Congress Cataloging-in-Publication Data

King, Alan, 1927–
  Is salami and eggs better than sex?

  1. Gastronomy—Anecdotes, facetiae, satire, etc.
I. Sheraton, Mimi. II. Title.
PN6231.G35K56   1985   641'.01'30207   85-15985
ISBN 0-316-49365-1

BP

*Published simultaneously in Canada
by Little, Brown & Company (Canada) Limited*

PRINTED IN THE UNITED STATES OF AMERICA

In an age of uptight, health-obsessed dieters, this book is lovingly dedicated to all the happy eaters who just don't give a damn.

— M.S. and A.K.

CONTENTS

 PROLOGUE

This book really began about two years before the actual writing and is one of the happier results of my penchant for eavesdropping. Always unable to resist the conversations of interesting strangers, I was transfixed at lunch in the grill of the "21" Club to find that I was seated on a banquette next to my favorite comic, Alan King.

It was not the conversation King was having with an agent that intrigued me, but rather the way he interrupted his own conversation to shout directions to a captain who was preparing steak tartare.

The friend I was eating with had a hard time getting my attention as I tried to follow the intricate instructions King was dishing out.

Although, as I later learned, he read the columns I wrote on food and restaurants in The New York Times, *Alan King did not recognize me, a tribute perhaps to my attempts at anonymity. As so often happened, the only person in the room who knew me (besides my friend, of* course) was one of the restaurant owners, Sheldon Tannen.

Not famous for his soft voice or his low-key delivery, Alan King was providing a floor show not only for me, but for the entire room.

The captain had the ingredients and condiments that would be mixed into the raw ground beef on an oval platter together with a few of the house's special touches. As he prepared to add each ingredient to the mixing bowl, he glanced at King to see if the latest candidate would be approved or rejected. A nod indicated that raw egg yolk was to go into the large white bowl, followed by tricklings of olive oil, Worcestershire sauce, lemon juice and a dab of English mustard. After whisking those liquids together with a fork, the captain added the meat, the capers, the salt and pepper and minced onion. As he turned to the minced white and yolk of hard-boiled egg, King stopped him: "No yolk. Only the white. And no anchovy."

I was so absorbed in the proceedings that I felt as though I was part of them, so the rejection of the anchovy came as a shock. "No anchovy?" I burst in, leaning over. "It really should have anchovy."

The sudden sound of my own voice jolted me into the realization of what I had done. Something in me braced against a maelstrom.

The room became almost hushed, no small feat in a setting as noisy as this one. The captain held his fork and spoon in a midair freeze, staring at the unexpected direction from which the query had come. King took off the half glasses over which he had been peering, leaned back against the banquette and pursed his lips as he turned slowly and inexorably toward me.

"Lady," he said, "you take care of your lunch and I'll take care of mine. For your information, I saw a Jacques Cousteau special last night and I'm giving up fish, especially with meat. And — not that it's any of your business, but I'll warn you now so you can get a grip on yourself — this steak tartare is going to be cooked." No stage whispers here, just a controlled blast.

"Cooked? Steak tartare?" I asked, unable to contain my surprise.

"Medium rare," was the answer, as much to the captain as to me.

I can't remember what I had for lunch that day, but I know it tasted a lot like crow. I slinked out soon after, still flushed with embarrassment. As I learned later, Alan King then asked Sheldon Tannen, "Who was that pushy yenta who put her two cents into my steak tartare?"

"That was Mimi Sheraton," Tannen said.

Two hours later there was a phone call at my office. It was Alan King. "Say, thanks for the advice. How much anchovy would you put into that much ground beef and would you chop it, or what?"

"Mash it," I managed to answer. "One fillet to about seven ounces of beef and rinse the anchovy first so it won't be too salty."

After that there were regular phone calls asking for recipes for roast chicken, sautéed potatoes with garlic or for stuffed breast of veal. Sometimes it was a request for a restaurant recommendation. Gradually it became obvious that it was indeed Alan King who did the cooking at home when there was no professional cook on hand, and that it was he and not his wife who planned the menus and who chose the restaurants.

It occurred to me that he would be an interesting subject for a food profile, and he agreed to be interviewed. It was accomplished over lunch at Il Nido, and as he talked about losing weight and ate his way through a plateful of tortellini heavily glossed with butter, cream and cheese and described the duck he expected to have at La Grenouille for dinner, I knew I was talking to a serious eater.

The resultant story, with food memories of his boyhood in the Williamsburg section of Brooklyn, and his meals with show-business personalities in restaurants all over the world, was the forerunner of this book.

Our weekly meetings in his Fifth Avenue office took on aspects of sessions with a psychoanalyst. Food is considered to be an innocent and benign topic, and when discussing it most people relax. They are, therefore, more revealing than they might be when on guard, and personalities and temperaments are clearly in view.

During each two- to three-hour session, I drank water and he drank gin.* We both drank because we were dieting, but though we tried to avoid food, we became ravenous talking about it. Sometimes we were driven to having emergency reinforcements of hot dogs sent up from Paley Park across the street, and once we ordered in so much corned beef from the Carnegie Deli that the desk seemed adrift in it.

---

* Know now that when the word "gin" appears in this book, as it often does, Gordon's is the gin referred to. It is the brand distributed by Renfield Importers, in which Alan King is a stockholder, and so, as he says, "What other gin would I drink?"

Alan King revealed himself to be, above all, a man who wants things the way he wants them, whether it is the special quarter-pound hot dogs custom-made for him by Hebrew National and which went back three times until they were the right length and thickness, or the steak tartare at "21." Or, I suspect, a table setting, a room, a script or a film that he is producing. Because he does so many things with an extraordinary amount of nervous energy, he has little patience, and when cooking, he prefers quick, visible combinations of basic ingredients rather than dishes that depend on complicated handwork. But he does like elaborate dishes in restaurants and rarely goes out for steak. "I like there to be some preparation involved," he says. "Something I won't or can't do myself."

Annoyed at pretentiousness, he does like beautiful restaurants ("I'll sacrifice some cooking skill for lovely surroundings and a friendly staff").

Warned against collaborating with a show-business star by writer friends who had bad experiences along those lines, I was braced for problems. I was told that anyone so occupied with pressures and exigencies would not really contribute to such a book, and that once bored by it, he would expect it to be ghostwritten.

I needn't have worried. I suspect that this became Alan King's pet project and was, in fact, his way of relaxing. I became aware, early on, that his wife, Jeanette, has a broad range of interests of her own, but food was definitely not among them and I began to think that King was starved for food talk. I began to feel like a gastronomic hetaera, there to satisfy his desire to discuss recipes, restaurants, food products and people. If he

called to change an appointment or give me some missing piece of information, he invariably took time out to
tell me what (and how) he had made for dinner the
night before. If I described a recipe we would include in
the book, he would go home and try it again to see if I
had it right. He was so dedicated to cooking that when
he had something he liked in a restaurant, he was not
above going back into the kitchen to see exactly how it
was done. And one night he saw Julia Child on television preparing a stuffed pot roast and he ran out the
next day, bought all the ingredients, prepared the roast
and then realized he had to find twelve people to eat it.
"She wasn't kidding with that name, stuffed braised
beef Gargantua," he says. "It's a good thing the gar-
dener was working that day and that the United Parcel
man came along."

As I listened to Alan King talk about his wife, I
realized that I was dealing with an almost unrecon-
structed male chauvinist. When Alan King says that
Jeanette had nothing to do all day, he means she had
nothing to do for him, and when he says, "You know
how 'they' argue," the "they" in his mind is women. I
suspect that his idea of being pro-feminist is to make a
pass at Gloria Steinem.

There is an obvious irony in Jeanette King's eating
habits. She is a near-vegetarian, straying from a diet of
tofu, alfalfa sprouts and yogurt only occasionally for
chicken or fish, and more often for Mallomars, Oreos
and Yodels. "She lives on fungus and junk food," King
reports. "My refrigerator looks as though it should be
sprayed with a weed killer. At times it even gets danger-
ous. I once got up for my three-o'clock-in-the-morning
snack and found very little food in the refrigerator —

*just some sort of nice-looking, white creamy cheese. I
took a mouthful and immediately knew I had made a
mistake. I ran upstairs screaming that I had been poi-
soned. Jeanette said it was something called whey
cheese. I called it solidified Kaopectate."*

There is, in fact, a sort of culinary polarization
within the King household. Elainie, their teenage
daughter, eats as her mother does, while their two sons,
Robert and Andy, follow their father's taste in food. In
fact, Robert King shares that interest in food so strongly
that he studied to become a chef at the Culinary Insti-
tute of America in Hyde Park, New York.

When calling for restaurant reservations Alan
orders a veal chop, duck or a rack of lamb for himself.
Jeanette calls later to be sure there will be steamed vegetables for her. Those given to psychological conjecture
might theorize that because she is married to a man
with such a strong and at times overpowering personal-
ity, Jeanette King, by refusing to share his menus, re-
tains not only her slim figure, but her identity as
well.

Most of this book, I trust, will explain itself, but
there seems to be some need to explain the title. Gram-
marians will cavil (some already have) about the sin-
gular verb "is" being used with what looks like the
plural subject "salami and eggs." That just shows how
much they know about salami and eggs (not to be confused with eggs and salami or salami with eggs). Beginning as separate ingredients, the salami and eggs
prepared in the standard fashion at all New York
kosher-style delis are combined into a single pancake
omelet, inset with slices of garlic-laden Eastern Euro-

pean sausage. Salami and eggs merge and then emerge
as a single subject. If you doubt that, go to the Carnegie
Delicatessen, order salami and eggs and then let us
know if you think the title of this book should be "Are
salami and eggs better than sex?" As for the answer to
that question, read on.

 ## STEAK TARTARE, MEDIUM RARE

FOR EACH SERVING
    In a large mixing bowl, combine 1 raw egg yolk,
which you beat lightly with a fork, about ½ teaspoon of
olive oil, a few drops each of lemon juice and Worcestershire sauce and a dab of prepared English mustard.
Blend with the fork until smooth.
    Add 6 to 7 ounces freshly ground raw beef trimmed
of all fat (fillet is perfect for this but sirloin will do)
and gently turn it through the liquid seasonings. Add a
scant teaspoon of well-drained capers, a teaspoon each
of finely minced raw onion and the minced white and
yolk of a hard-boiled egg and a generous pinch of
chopped parsley. Mash one rinsed anchovy fillet and
turn that into the meat mixture. Add salt and freshly
ground black pepper to taste. Do not add salt before adding the anchovy. Gently shape into an oval patty, being
careful not to pack the meat too firmly.
    Heat 1 tablespoonful unsalted butter in an iron, a
copper or an enameled cast-iron skillet, and when bubbling subsides, add the meat. Sauté briefly, turning once
so both sides become golden brown and the center is medium rare. Serve on a piece of toast that may be rubbed
lightly with garlic and then buttered.

SALAMI AND EGGS

FOR EACH SERVING

Start with kosher-style salami that is about 3½ to 4 inches in diameter. This should be sliced by hand, with a sharp knife, to a thickness of ⅛ inch. You will need 4 slices. Cut three or four small notches around the edge of each slice so that it will not curl or buckle during cooking.

Using an 8 to 9-inch black iron skillet (Teflon-lined, if you're still in amateur ranks), heat about 1 tablespoon of unsalted butter and a teaspoon of mild salad oil. Add the salami slices and fry slowly, turning once, so that slices take on a thin crusty glaze on both sides.

Beat 3 eggs lightly with a fork and add a small pinch of salt and a generous grinding of black pepper. When salami slices are brown on both sides, add a small pat of butter to the pan, and when it has melted, pour in eggs over salami.

Fry slowly over moderate heat, pulling cooked edges of omelet inward so uncooked portion can run out into the pan. Continue until top is firm and bottom is light golden brown and can be freed easily from the pan.

Have a 10-inch dinner plate nearby. When the first side of the omelet is cooked, invert it onto the plate, cooked side up. Then slide the omelet back into the pan, uncooked side down, adding a tiny piece of butter first if the pan seems dry. The second side will become golden brown in less time than the first side.

Serve on a warm plate. For garnish, Alan King thinks you should trickle a thin circle of ketchup *around the omelet, about an inch and a half in from the edge. I say, save the ketchup for french fries but have the salami and eggs with some delicatessen mustard. We both agree that a toasted bialy should be eaten with this, but Alan suggests a half-sour pickle. Trust me and ask for a full sour.*

CHAPTER ONE

Coming Home

Often a book takes on a life of its own as it is being written. Conscious of documenting experiences and making them entertaining, the author instinctively reexamines daily activities to see what impression they would make in print, and perhaps at times even adjusts actions so they will "read" better.

As we worked on this book, Alan King began to notice even more than usual, how and what he cooked and ate, and what his taste preferences really were. When I teased him about adding sautéed green peppers and onions to every dish he cooked, he said nothing. Then, a week later, he announced that he had made dinner every night without once using green peppers and onions. He also gave up non-stick pans, and practiced until he mastered the art of getting pancakes and omelets off iron pans as professionals do.

In much the same way the book began to insinuate itself into the life of the family. One result is the story that follows, almost verbatim as he told it the day after it happened, striding around his office exactly as he strides around a stage and with characteristic gestures — jutting the lower jaw, pulling one shoulder back, chomping on a cigar — that indicate Alan King was definitely "on."

YOU KNOW, THIS HAS BEEN A GOOD summer so far for Jeanette and me. There were lots of nice parties in July and we didn't have any major fights, only a series of minor disagreements. She's been eating almost normally. One weekend she had a lot of that great jambalaya made by John Steinbeck's widow, Elaine, at her house in Sag Harbor, and then she even ate barbecued lamb at George Plimpton's in East Hampton. It's been nice having eating company for a change. We've even been able to discuss the same dishes, like a regular couple. We've been married for thirty-eight years and went out for five years before, and so for forty-three years that's almost never happened. Please understand that I met Jeanette when she was five. I cannot imagine life without her even though she is a vegetarian and always dieting, so that we never eat the same meals.

Right now we don't have a cook, so yesterday morning Jeanette says to me, "Tell me what you want to cook for dinner and I'll shop and prepare everything for you."

That may not sound so unusual, but you have

to realize that if it weren't necessary to walk through the kitchen to get to the garage, my wife would never set foot in the room. When she says "prepare" food, that doesn't mean cooking it. It means buying and cleaning it, chopping or cutting it and laying it all out so that when I get there everything is ready and I can start cooking. I like to have food set out like a patient who has been prepped for surgery.

I realized she was making up for the night before.

We had had a date for dinner at the Four Seasons and I took a change of clothes to the office so I could shower and dress there. When I put my shirt on at six o'clock, I realized it had French cuffs and I did not bring cuff links. I called every store in the neighborhood, but they were all closed. I called Jeanette at the house and, sure enough, she was just about ready to leave. I just caught her. I asked her to bring my gold bamboo cuff links to the restaurant and she said fine.

I folded my sleeves up so the cuffs wouldn't show, put on my jacket and walked over to my neighborhood pub, "21." I usually do that — stand at the bar, have a drink, kill time and see who's around.

I stopped for matches at the cigarette counter and met Pete Kriendler, who was just leaving. He looks at my wrists and says, "Alan? A short-sleeved shirt?" Of course, I hate that look almost more than anything, so I quickly explained about the cuff links.

Pete insists that I take his cuff links because he was going home and wouldn't need them. I said Jeanette was bringing mine, but he wouldn't take no for an answer and so I put on his links — they were gold telephone dials that really turned. I went into the bar and met Ken Venturi, the golfer and sportscaster, and right off, he admires the cuff links.

When it was time, I took a slow walk over to the Four Seasons and Jeanette was there. I ask for the cuff links and she slaps her forehead and says, "My God! I forgot them. But," she says, acting relieved, "I see you have some anyway." With us that night were Sue and Herman Merinoff — he's the chairman of the board of Renfield. To say the least, both are dear, quiet, low-profile people. But try as I might, I could feel myself getting steamed.

"What's my having cuff links got to do with it?" I said, or more probably, yelled. "My having them is not the point. You forgetting them is. Were they too heavy for you? Was it too much to ask you to bring them here? What did you do today, exercise and play tennis? With so much exercise you should be in the Olympics. With all that tennis, you should be at Wimbledon." By now, of course, the whole place is staring at me.

I turned to a man at the bar who could not help overhearing all of this and I said, "Sir? You look like an impartial observer. Let me ask you. Do you think it is too much to ask a wife who is home all day to bring her husband's cuff links to dinner?"

The poor guy was so embarrassed he mumbled, "I'm from out of town." And he left.

Anyway, back to yesterday morning. Jeanette had made a friendly offer, so I thought about the weekend during which we had done some pretty heavy eating and I tried to plan a sort of diet-type menu that Jeanette would enjoy. I asked her to pick some of the really ripe tomatoes from the garden and to cut them in chunks. Then I told her to buy green peppers and to cut them in long slivers and to have onions coarsely chopped and garlic finely minced. For the main course we would have chicken breasts — bone in and skin on so they stay juicy and have flavor — and I planned to sauté them in a little olive oil and butter with some herbs and white wine. I would add a few sausages to that for myself. I also asked for some broccoli, which I figured I'd sauté in olive oil with a touch of garlic. Nice and al dente. She likes that.

We settled all of this at six in the morning because by six-thirty I wanted to be on my way out to New Jersey where I had a meeting with my son Andy, who wanted to talk to me about his automobile business. Anyway, I always plan dinner first thing in the morning. That's the only way I can get through the day, having a specific meal to look forward to at night. And I never settle for a "We'll see . . ." about dinner. There are no "We'll sees" about my food.

Well, the day got really hot and crazy for me. After Jersey, I had to get back to New York for a ses-

sion with Bruce Fierstein, whom I'm writing a
movie script with, and then I had to be at an important meeting at Kaufman-Astoria Studios in
Queens. In between, I kept in touch with the office
to put out fires there. I got home twelve hours after I
left.

Everything looked peaceful and beautiful when
I got there. Jeanette had all the ingredients set out
in nice little bowls and, I'll tell you, even the kitchen
looked especially good. The Spanish tiles were shining, all of my favorite knives and pans were set out
near the Garland stove and it looked ready to go. The
table was set on the porch and there were fresh
roses from our garden in a big glass bowl and the
sky was all red from the sunset over Long Island
Sound and the twilight was blue and sort of shim-
mering.

Jeanette had set out a tray and on it was a bottle of gin, club soda, ice, sliced limes and a glass —
all for me. There was a dish of broccoli flowerets and
another of green pepper strips and a curry dip.
Jeanette was even wearing an apron. "That's terrific!" I said, and kissed her.

So I fix myself a drink and begin to get ready
for the cooking. After I took off my jacket, put on
comfortable pants and my tennis shoes, I munch on
some vegetables and sip my drink. Jeanette is having a glass of white wine, and I pull out the sauté
pan large enough to hold the four chicken breasts,
another pan for the peppers, tomatoes and onions,
and a pot for the broccoli.

Then I look at the garlic and see it is not minced, as I asked, but that it's in whole cloves. Then I notice that the onions are sliced, not coarsely chopped. Even so, things are going smoothly, so I just quietly remark that I had wanted the garlic minced and the onions chopped. "Oh, I didn't know," she says. "Anyway," she adds, "how do I get the garlic and onion chopped in just certain ways?"

So I got out a big old-fashioned wooden chopping bowl and one of those half-moon choppers and I said I would do it while she got flour that I could use to dust the chicken before I sauté it.

I'm chopping away, thinking that she really should have done this since she volunteered. But, what the hell. It's her first time as sous-chef. Next, I turned to the chicken to flour it and damned if I could find the flour.

"Where's the flour?" I asked.

"I thought you had used it already, so I put it away," she said.

"How could you think I used it?" I asked, trying to stay calm. "Don't you know what used flour looks like? If you cooked, you would know that used flour has dents in it and there is usually a light sprinkling around the counter." But I got hold of myself and said, "Okay. Let's start all over. But for God's sake, don't clean anything." I can't stand it when they clean up after me while I'm still cooking — always pulling utensils away to wash them and mopping up counters and using the sink when I need it.

I began to get ready to cook and wanted to line up all the ingredients. I asked for the broccoli and green peppers. "You're eating them," she said.

"You mean to say that you let me eat the broccoli and green peppers? They were not for crudités. They were for cooking. I thought we were eating extras!" By now I knew I was coming to a boil even if dinner wasn't.

Now we're both getting sore but are still going back and forth between counter, sink and stove, me sipping gin and Jeanette still on white wine and I'm preparing the food without missing a beat.

"Could I have some olive oil and butter for the chicken?" I ask her.

"Why don't you use safflower oil and margarine?" she asks.

"Because I don't like safflower oil and margarine," I answer.

I smash two cloves of garlic and put them in the oil and butter and start to brown the chicken. I put what's left of the broccoli in another pot and the remains of the peppers with the onions in another. I hand Jeanette two wooden spoons and ask her to stir the vegetables just enough to keep them from burning while they are sautéing.

I glance over to see how it's going and i notice that she's hardly stirring at all and that the vegetables will almost surely burn. She's just holding the wooden spoon handles lightly between her thumb and forefinger — carefully, so she won't spoil her manicure.

"Don't kitzle it," I say. "Stir it as though you mean it. Really hold the handles of the spoons." Next thing I know, there's oil and vegetables all over the floor in front of the stove. She not only stirred it; she beat the hell out of it, probably wishing it were me she had in those pans.

"For God's sake, look at that mess," I say. "You know these tennis shoes are made for clay courts, not oil slick. I'll break my neck sliding in that."

"Too bad," she says, looking strangely cheerful. "You said not to clean anything and I won't clean this." I tell her that if she ever cooks again she ought to put newspapers on the floor, like my mother always did on Friday nights.

"You fix your own goddam peppers," she screams.

I wondered why she was angry.

Meanwhile, I finish browning the chicken and I've preheated the oven to 200 degrees so I can keep it hot and let the grease drain off. Then I realized I needed a little white wine to deglaze the pan. I always keep an open bottle in the refrigerator for cooking; I hate to open a new bottle for just a few tablespoons. But the only white wine in sight was in Jeanette's glass and that had an ice cube in it. It was more water than wine. Then I realized that she had been drinking my cooking wine.

I became more furious than ever and so did she, but we both continued putting this meal together, slamming things as we went along.

I opened a new bottle of white wine, figuring

we would have it with dinner, but the cork was all ferschimmelt and it crumbled into the wine. I ask Jeanette to strain the wine and while I'm watching three pots, I see out of the corner of my eye that she's spilling the wine. I naturally say something like, "You're spilling the wine."

She says something like, "This is the last time I'm ever going to help you in the kitchen." (Never mind that it is practically the first.) "I'm not your sommelier," she adds.

Then she says, "You know something? You're a Hitler in the kitchen. Ever since you began working on that goddam book, you think you know how everything should taste. If you want to know something, I hate your food, I hate you and I hate Mimi Sheraton."

Now I begin to go to pieces. I've had three glasses of gin, I'm starved, the day has been a bitch and I look in my apron pocket and find an empty cigarette pack. I open the drawer where we keep extra packs and there's nothing there.

Again I try to stay calm. "Jeanette," I say. "Jeanette, when I gave you the shopping list this morning, didn't it include a carton of Merits?"

"Oh, I forgot," she says. "But anyway, smoking's not good for you."

Then I explode. "What's not good for me is not what this is about. What it's about is that you don't smoke so you forget cigarettes. You don't eat so you don't cook. You don't wear French cuffs so you forget the goddam cuff links."

Then it's her turn to explode. "Take the chicken and shove it up your ass," she screams. "I'm not eating!" With that, she picks up the bowl of tomatoes and says, "You want tomatoes? Here are your lousy tomatoes!" And with that, she throws the tomatoes into the garbage pail.

Then I take two breasts of chicken out of the oven — her portion — and I throw those in the garbage pail. Now there are just my two breasts of chicken and the sliced sausages I'm sautéing for myself.

Next, she takes some of the peppers and onions and tosses those into the pail with some of my sausages. By now, the garbage is beginning to look pretty good and I'm thinking, maybe I'll bake it in the bag, en papillote.

Then I begin to scream that I'm having a nicotine fit complete with withdrawal symptoms and I even try to find a butt in an ashtray. But that doesn't do it.

Finally we settle down at the table with the roses on it and now there are only two pieces of chicken and some scraps of other stuff. I share it all with Jeanette but she just sits there, not touching it. She just watches me eat. Punishing me. When I saw she wasn't going to eat at all, I took her plate and finished it.

"You're an animal," she kept mumbling as I ate. "An animal."

By now I'm crazy to have a cigarette and she offers to go and get some for me — sort of to make up for forgetting. I said, "I'll go with you." So we leave everything all over the kitchen and drive to the candy store in town and damned if the place isn't closed. This is really not my night! So we go on to a pharmacy and I decide that while I'm there, I'll get a few things I need, like shaving cream and toothpaste. But I look around and see that the shelves are three-quarters empty. I wanted five things and they are out of four. I yell out, "What the hell kind of store is this, anyway? There's no merchandise. No wonder the discount stores are beating the hell out of you guys."

Of course, the store is pretty quiet by that time of night, but the few customers and clerks there are all staring at us. Jeanette looks at one clerk and says, "Don't let him bother you. I've had to put up with this maniac all during dinner."

"Maniac?" I ask the clerk. "Why don't you ask her about the cuff links and the cigarettes and the broccoli?"

As we leave the store, Jeanette says, "I need dessert. Let's get some frozen custard."

Meat she won't eat, but frozen custard she needs. I tell her I'll get her the custard but that I won't eat that crap. So she gets a frozen custard cone and as she gets back into the car, the whole thing topples down onto the upholstery. I start to laugh and she asks me how come I'm not mad about that. "Because, sweetie, it's your car," I answer.

But that wasn't all. Driving home, I go through a yellow warning light and, sure enough, there's a cop motioning me to pull over. He asks for my license and while I'm getting it, I try to explain. "Well, you see, officer, sir, I've had a very trying day and night . . ."

Meanwhile, Jeanette sidles close to me and whispers, "Why don't you open your big mouth to *him*?"

"I may be crazy, but I'm not stupid!" I answer.

That did it and we both started to laugh. We suddenly realized how ridiculous the whole evening had been.

When we got home, Jeanette said, "I just remembered. We have some marvelous double dark chocolate ice cream in the freezer." And so we took it up to bed, turned on the television and each of us finished a quart of ice cream.

 ## CHICKEN AND SAUSAGES EN PAPILLOTE, À LA GARBAGE

SERVES 4 TO 8

Cooking, like science, has its happy accidents. This dish, devised with what went into the King garbage on that fateful night, is a perfect example. All of the sautéing can be done in advance and the browned ingredients can be folded into the aluminum foil and baked just before serving.

Have the butcher split 4 whole chicken breasts in half. Skin and bones should remain. Slice 4 hot or sweet Italian sausages into two or three pieces. Place 3 tablespoons butter and 3 tablespoons olive oil in a large heavy skillet. When hot, add sausage pieces. Brown slowly on all sides; remove and reserve.

Lightly dust chicken pieces with flour and brown a few at a time in the hot fat. Remove and reserve.

Put 2 large green peppers that have been seeded and cut in long slivers, 2 coarsely chopped large onions, 2 minced garlic cloves and a generous pinch of oregano in the pan. Sauté slowly, adding butter or oil as needed until vegetables begin to wilt.

Stir in 6 fresh skinned and chopped tomatoes, or a 1-pound can of well-drained chopped tomatoes. Simmer until sauce is slightly thickened — about 10 minutes. Pour into bowl.

Add 1 cup dry white wine to the empty pan and, over high heat, let wine come to a boil. Using a wooden spatula, scrape all coagulated pan juices into wine. Let wine reduce by half.

Prepare a sheet of heavy-duty aluminum foil that is about 24 inches long. Place this in a shallow baking pan about 9 x 12 inches. Preheat the oven to 350 degrees. Place the browned chicken breasts in the center of the foil, overlapping them a bit so there is a margin of foil at the sides.

Top the chicken with the sausages, then spoon on the pepper, onions and tomatoes and the wine sauce. Finally add a handful of chopped parsley and 8 or 10 fresh basil leaves. Bring the edges of the foil together and pinch them closed on all sides.

Bake in oven for 30 to 40 minutes, the time depending on how hot the ingredients were to begin with. You can open the foil to see if the chicken breasts are done. If they're not, seal the edges again and continue baking.

To serve, slide the unopened foil packet onto a

*large platter and take it to the table, to be opened there
so that guests can enjoy the aroma.*

This amount will serve four to eight people, depending on their appetites. Steamed rice or any cooked,
drained, short tubular pasta, such as penne or ziti,
would be very good with this. Spoon chicken, sausages
and sauce over a bed of the rice or pasta.

 JAMBALAYA

SERVES 6 TO 8

Slice 2 pounds of hot Italian or Spanish Chorizo
sausages into 1½-inch-thick pieces. Brown slowly in a
little olive oil in a cast-iron or enameled cast-iron Dutch
oven. Remove and reserve.

Add 4 tablespoons of olive oil to the fat in the pan
and when it is hot, add two finely chopped green peppers and two chopped large onions. Add 3 or 4 minced
garlic cloves and sauté slowly until vegetables are wilted
but not brown.

Stir in 1½ pounds of diced cooked ham and continue sautéing until ingredients are light golden brown.
Add 1 teaspoon salt, ½ teaspoon black pepper, ½ teaspoon crumbled leaf thyme and 2 large bay leaves. Sauté
for a few seconds, then pour in two 1-pound cans of tomatoes with their liquid. Add 1 cup of water and bring
to a boil.

Add the sausages to the pot and simmer for about
30 minutes, or until sausages are done and sauce is beginning to thicken. Add 2½ pounds peeled shrimp and
simmer for another 15 minutes, adding water if sauce
becomes too thick and sticks to the pot.

Traditionally, rice is added to this sauce and cooks

with the other ingredients, but if you want to prepare this in advance and serve it to guests, it is better to cook the rice separately and add it to the sauce during the reheating. Cook 3 cups long-grain converted rice for about 10 minutes. Drain. Half an hour before serving, add the rice to the other ingredients and heat together for 20 to 30 minutes. If you like very hot seasonings, you can add a pinch of cayenne or a few drops of Tabasco sauce to the other ingredients, but proceed cautiously, as the sausages will add their flavor to the sauce.

CHAPTER TWO

 # You'll Eat,
You'll Feel Better

As so many successful literary collaborations prove, it is not necessary for the participants to have shared the same background. My experience with this book, however, indicates that it certainly helps. At times when Alan King was recalling experiences of his childhood, I thought he might have been reading from my own autobiographical cookbook, From My Mother's Kitchen. *So many recollections matched mine, undoubtedly because we both grew up Jewish in Brooklyn at exactly the same time — between the Depression and World War II. We could, and often did, finish each other's sentences, much to the consternation of Leslie Kern, Alan's secretary, who patiently transcribed the tapes.*

There were some differences, of course. Alan King lived in Williamsburg while I was in Flatbush. My mother was born in Brooklyn, his mother came from Lithuania. In practical terms, that simply meant my mother was assimilated enough to skim the fat off chicken soup: his mother still thought that the fat was the best part. He said "bagel" and I said "beigel," but whether the pronunciation was Litvakian (his) or Galitzian (mine), we both remember that tough and chewy boil-and-bake roll as the cornerstone of a monumental Sunday breakfast based on enough salty belly lox to keep us drinking water all day long.

The phenomenon of food as a symbol of love and nurturing is not restricted to Jews. It is equally familiar to Italians, Germans, Irish, Chinese and any other group close to its ethnic roots. It was that enveloping (indeed, often suffocating) warmth that Alan King credits with keeping him on the straight and narrow path. Otherwise, he conjectures, he might have followed in the footsteps of his neighborhood's only prosperous members — the big-time spender gangsters with flashy cars and star-sapphire pinky rings who afforded him his first glimpse of what looked like the better life.

As I listened to Alan King, I recognized other familiar aspects of our childhoods. Notice how often the word "yelled" appears where most people would use "said." Nothing got "said" in those households; it was always yelled. And what they yelled was a lightning repartée, a give and take that placed a premium on the swift retort and, above all, on the importance of being funny.

Psychologists Dr. Rod Martin and Dr. Herbert Lefcourt of the University of Waterloo in Ontario, Canada, recently found in experiments for a forthcoming book that humor often is a buffer between stress and negative moods — a successful way to cope with adversity. Small wonder, then, that people whose entire lives were *exercises in adversity would have developed humor as an antidote.*

The only time Alan King really lost his temper during this project came in the course of this chapter. As he was describing how his mother made chremsleth, the Passover matzo meal pancakes, I asked if she beat the egg whites separately so the pancakes would be light.

He pulled off his glasses, slammed his hand down on his desk and yelled, "I told you that in my mother's cooking there was no such thing as light! You don't listen!"

I WAS BORN ON THE TWENTY-FIFTH OF December. In my house that was the fourth day of Chanukah, never mind what it meant on the standard calendar. The closest thing we had to a Santa Claus was my white-bearded, sainted rabbigrandfather — my mother's father. He was not exactly a saint and his beard was not exactly white. The lower part of the mustache and the upper part of the beard were turning a rich burnt sienna, a result of his smoking five packs of Murad cigarettes every day until he died at a hundred and four. And he didn't even die of natural causes. He was shot by a jealous lover. Surgeon General, please note!

Although I was a child of the Depression, I never knew we were poor until I got rich. We were on what was then called "relief," a better word than welfare because it sounds like temporary help. Welfare sounds as though it's good for you. We moved a lot to take advantage of the two or three months' rent concessions that were standard then, but the apartment I remember best was at 295 South Second Street. It was a dingy, cold-water railroad flat one flight up over the grocery store. That's where the nearest telephone was, and if anyone called us, they'd yell up from the store and we would go down. Everyone sat out on the stoop of that house except my mother. She looked out of the front window, leaning on a pillow, waiting for automobile accidents. After all, there was no television and no soap operas to watch.

I don't know what the official names for our rooms were, like parlor and dining room. To us they were just a kitchen and bedrooms and a foyer. The kitchen was huge and had a big oak table and usually enough seats for between ten and twelve people. Seats, not necessarily chairs. Sometimes we pulled up boxes and orange crates when we had company. Once in a while the landlord would come in to look around and he'd say, "Ah! How lovely to be in this Garden of Eden!" My mother's instant comeback was, "Next year, how much are you going to want for these five black holes?"

My name then was Irwin Alan Kniberg. My father always said that the *K* was silent, like the *Q* in billiards. My mother still calls me Irwin in private. In public, she calls me Alanking. To her, that's one word.

My father came from Warsaw, and my mother said he was the first Polish joke. He had sophisticated tastes in food and ate everything, including lobster, which he could pick clean, meticulously. But he never had that food at home because my mother has always been strictly kosher. To her, pork is a four-letter word. She was born in a shtetl near Vilna in Lithuania. She used to tell us horrible stories about cossacks and pogroms. She never knew she had so much fun as a child until she saw *Fiddler on the Roof.* "Who had time for all that dancing and singing?" she asked. "All I remember is a lot of hiding."

But as poor as we were, there was always food on the table and clean tablecloths, and we always had fresh bedding and plenty of blankets even though we slept three kids to a bed. I had six brothers and one sister. All of them were smart and always in some sort of school or other. One brother was even an intern. I was the only one who hated school. My mother used to say I had no sitz fleisch — sitting flesh.

Food was what our lives revolved around. That's why the kitchen was, in the strictest sense, our living room and why my mother was always in it. But even her ordinarily heavy cooking schedule didn't compare to the year's biggest culinary extravaganza, Passover, the holiday during which we reflect on the saga of the Jews' flight out of bondage in Egypt. One Passover stands out in my mind as The Saga of My Grandfather's Foot.

That hectic week of shopping, scrubbing and planning began as usual, if you can call it usual to find the family's only bathtub filled with pots and dishes soaking in salt water one day, and a big fish swimming in it the next. The dishes were soaked to be made "clean" for Passover. Those who could afford it, had two sets of dishes — one for Passover and another for the rest of the year. Of course, if you were kosher, that meant four sets of everything. Those who couldn't afford separate sets were permitted to do the salt-water soaking. When the dishes came out of the tub, the carp went in. If you watched carefully, you might be able to get into the bath before the fish. The carp was bought live so he would be fresh for the gefilte fish. We couldn't afford real pets, either, so whenever there was a fish in the tub, we gave it a name and played games with it. When my mother killed it, one of the kids was sure to yell, "How can you eat anything that has a first name?"

One morning, just as my mother was in the midst of preparations, my grandfather came out of his bedroom, dragging one leg as he walked. My mother noticed it but didn't want to seem too concerned and frighten him. "Zaideh probably slept on it," she said, half to herself. She went to the store and began her usual performance as a combination purchasing agent and director. She liked food from special parts of the animal, the container or the store. It was her form of geography. "Take it from the back. Cut it from the middle. Reach down to the bottom of the barrel." She thought something remote was better, because the storekeeper would

put the worst things up front to sell them first. And
as always, she told the butcher, "Throw in a piece
liver for the cat." I was the cat.

Even at Passover, nobody shopped with cash.
There wasn't any. "I'll pay you Friday," was the
line. Mrs. Sigofsky, the grocer, wrote down what you
owed her in a big black book with a thick pencil
stub. We always managed to pay those bills somehow. My father sewed cuffs and belts on an old
Singer sewing machine that had a foot treadle. He
also sold Hooverettes, the wrap-around aprons
named after Herbert Hoover. "Another brain surgeon they put in the White House," he said.

Everything but the vegetables and cake came
from the grocer or butcher. Horseradish, parsley,
soup greens and so on were bought from a street
peddler, and cake came from Dugan's Day-Old Bakery. We could still eat those cakes the week before
Passover, and my mother would heat them in the
oven and say they were healthier than the fresh. She
never mentioned cheaper.

After school, I went home to help with the Passover cleaning because I was the youngest. While I
hung around the kitchen, I kidded my mother about
her cooking, a habit I picked up from my father. He
always teased her about food. "Minnie, you must
have made a mistake. It's not bad." He never said
good. And if he came home when she was making
sour milk, letting it ferment on the back of the stove,
he'd sniff for a second and then ask, "Who died?"

My favorite target was her chicken soup, especially when it was cold and had a lid of yellow fat on it. "Hey, Ma! I could ice-skate across that soup. And your matzo balls would make great hockey pucks." When she made matzo balls, she didn't know light and fluffy.

The next day, as I was leaning over the sink, having my favorite lunch — a sandwich of egg salad dripping with mayonnaise on a big kaiser roll — I could hear my grandfather's foot dragging as he walked. I asked my mother what was wrong. "Shhh. He's an old man," she whispered. "Last night I soaked the foot in Epsom salt, but it didn't help."

"Why don't you soak it in chicken soup?" I asked her.

"Save the jokes for your bums in the street," she said, striking out with a forehand like Ivan Lendl's, quickly followed by Jimmy Connors's backhand.

"Poppa, sit down at the table. You'll eat, you'll feel better," she said to my grandfather. My mother thought food cured everything. Her pharmacopoeia included not only soup but honey and lemon juice for coughs, warm tea bags for a toothache, freshly grated horseradish to be sniffed for a head cold, mustard plasters that blistered our chests and sacks of garlic she hung around our necks during infantile paralysis epidemics.

But even though she was worried, she kept right on with her preparations. As I look back, I don't know how she managed to do it all. Not only the ordinary shopping and cooking of meals for about twelve people, but the cleaning and shopping for Passover. She even had to feed the fish in the tub. She kept putting the new Passover foods in a big locked closet to keep them separate from the rest of the food. I had a job delivering milk every morning at six for a local grocery store and with the tips I got, I bought fresh rolls and brought them home for breakfast. Then on the way to school, I stopped at the synagogue where Zaideh worked, even with his bad foot, and took him a pot of boiled milk that had a skin on it. I hated the way the milk smelled, and the ploika — the skin — looked as if it stuck to his beard, but he thought that it was the best part. That, and the piece of salt herring and the spitzle, or end, of the rye bread. We used to fight over those ends and my mother said my sister always had to have one to be sure her first child would be a boy. (It worked.)

By the third day, my father got a cane for my grandfather and my mother was almost in tears, saying, "I don't know what to do next."

"Try a poultice of chicken fat," I said, still not taking her seriously. That time she reached me from across the room by swatting me with the end of a wet towel. She would reach out with whatever was in her hand, except a knife. Not that it would have mattered. She never had a sharp one. If Caesar had been stabbed with one of my mother's knives, we never would have heard the line "Et tu, Brute?"

I was also very good at chopping onions and making salmon salad and things like that because I had worked as a soda jerk and short-order cook in Diamond's Hickshop, a luncheonette across the street from Eastern District High School, where Jeanette went to school. I was fired when the owner realized that I was making huge sandwiches for my friends and charging them anything they had — a dime, a nickel, whatever. He suddenly realized that his place was always crowded but that he was losing money.

At home I also chopped the carrots and celery that my mother used for her terrific pot roast. Like everything else she made, it cooked for two days, but was it delicious! All that salt, pepper and garlic and the great potatoes that cooked along with it and soaked up the juices! I make a great daube of beef, but I swear it's not as good as her potted brisket. She says that's because I don't cook it long enough. Maybe, but who can stand around watching a stove for a whole weekend? She also did great boiled beef, but things like steaks and roasts were awful because the meat had to be koshered by being soaked in salt for hours. What salt does to ice, it also does to meat.

In addition to everything else on her mind, at Passover my mother had to think about the price of food, especially since there would be about twenty people to feed at two Seder dinners. That food was elaborate, and aunts, uncles and cousins would be coming from the Bronx and New Jersey and would be staying overnight.

Passover was a time of very special food. That's why the relief lady who went to homes unannounced to see how the money was being spent always visited Jewish homes on Fridays, and before Passover. She told my mother that she liked to come to our house best because it was so clean and cheerful and the food looked good even though it was cheap. She once asked my mother for her recipe for mushroom and barley soup.

But my mother also gave her a few lessons in economy cooking. She was her own Hamburger Helper, doing wonderful things with all sorts of starches, and especially before Passover when the noodles with cabbage or pot cheese or baked into puddings with apples and raisins, kasha and pasta flecks, known as farfel, had to be eaten or thrown away, because they were considered leavened or tainted.

My mother never cooked with recipes. If you watched, you learned. She belonged to the schitterein (throw in) school of cooking, no pun intended. I even knew how densely (very) I was supposed to pack the ground beef that went into karnetzlach, the sausage-shaped hamburgers. They were mixed with lots of raw garlic and pepper, and when they were broiled they got as hard as bullets. I once told her she should give her recipe to the OSS so they could provide karnetzlach kits to their agents. Then if they were captured behind German lines, they could swallow one of those instead of cyanide.

The day before Passover was the time for the ritual of sweeping up the symbolic chometz (ordinary foods forbidden at Passover), and it was usually my grandfather's job to go from room to room with a turkey feather, whisking up the food placed there into a bottle. But he just couldn't make it through the apartment. Finally I said to my mother, "Enough already with the witches' brews and the hot flannel packs of Nyafat and the camphorated oil. Your son Jack is an intern at Saint John's. Let's take Zaideh over there."

Those doctors got hold of that old man and started with X rays, tests, everything. Finally my brother came out and said he had a consultation with the other doctors. He carefully explained that the X rays don't show anything, but that wasn't important. He said that the real problem was old age and that there were calcium deposits, deteriorating musculature and maybe even gout. There was really nothing to do but take him home and give him aspirin and wrap his foot in an Ace bandage.

My father said that what my grandfather needed was a shot of schnapps. Whiskey was to him what chicken soup was to my mother. He took a shot of it for everything every morning at 6:00 A.M. and still does. Gets his heart going, he says. I can still hear that "Hotcha!" he let out as the whiskey went down. It always made my mother mad. "Bernie, how could you?" she'd say. How could he? My old man is ninety-four and he has been drinking since he was three.

The day of Passover began as it always did, with the making of the charoses (chopped apples, nuts

and wine) and the trimming of the horseradish for
the bitter herbs, which, my father said, were a
blessing because they killed the taste of the food. My
job was peeling the hard-boiled eggs that were to be
served in salt water. I was considered an egg specialist because when I was ten I had worked in a dairy
store, candling eggs. I held each egg up to a candle
flame to see if it had blood spots and was, therefore,
not good. The man I worked for was a monster who
had a forefinger like a poker, and he would jab it into
my shoulder when he told me what to do. One day I
asked for time off to go swimming in the new public
pool that had just opened, and he bawled me out.
When his finger was just about to go through my
flesh to the raw bone, I lost my temper. I picked up
all the rotten eggs and threw them into the electric
fan. That night, my father candled my ass.

It was some job setting the Passover table because it was more crowded than ever. It's a good
thing there was no place set for my mother. I never
saw her sit down to eat a meal. "After tasting all day
long, who feels like eating?" she said. My chair, as
always, was up against the icebox and because my
mother needed things during the meal, I had to get
up forty times. That icebox did a lot for our family,
not only by keeping our food cold, but also by keeping my parents together. My father's job was empty-
ing the drip pan underneath it. When he got really
mad and walked out, saying he'd never be back,
she'd say, "He'll be back. He has to empty the drip
pan." She was right.

As the relatives gathered before the Seder, they all noticed my grandfather's limp and started whispering, asking what was wrong. "Why are you all whispering?" my father asked. "Besides limping, he's also hard of hearing."

Fortunately you're supposed to eat leaning at the Passover table, and the head of the family does so symbolically. That night we leaned my grandfather's foot on a pillow on an extra chair. While the men were reading the Haggadah, literally, the "telling" of the Passover story, my mother was telling the story of the leg. My brother interrupted several times to repeat his diagnosis and my Uncle Hymie sat there, taking it all in. After dinner, Uncle Hymie helped my grandfather into his room and in five minutes, he came back into the kitchen holding up one of the high black shoes my grandfather wore. Looking at my brother the doctor, my uncle reached into the shoe and pulled out a sock that had been rolled up in the toe and forgotten. Chanting the diagnoses, "Gout! Calcium deposits! Old age!" he finished up with "Bullshit!"

Everyone had a good laugh, except my brother, but the medical crisis was not over. Having gorged myself on the gigantic meal, ending up with three of the chremsleth that were fried and soaked in cold honey until they were as tough as rubber gaskets, I woke up in the middle of the night with a terrible stomachache. Of course everyone ran into the room, including my brother Jack.

"Get him away from me," I yelled.

"Maybe he swallowed a sock," Uncle Hymie said.

"What he needs is a good cleaning out," my mother said, and I knew I was in for her last-ditch remedy — an enema. It was the only one she had not tried on my grandfather and she was probably frustrated. Her enema was of the genre known as a high colonic. Don't compare that to a Fleet. That can't even clean out a chicken. When my mother first saw a Fleet, she said it must be a mouthwash.

I remember lying on the bed on my stomach while my father got up on the dresser so he could hold that big porcelain pot high enough. In it was hot water and yellow floor soap that flowed through a rubber tube connected to a hollow plastic "bone." An enema was a family happening. Uncle Hymie held me down, because when that bone was shoved in I gagged. It cleared my sinuses, knocked the wax out of my ears and curled my hair. My father stood up there like the Statue of Liberty while my mother yelled, "Higher, Bernie! Higher!"

Meanwhile I was screaming and writhing and her standard line was, "Hold it in just a little more, just a little more. Take a deep breath." She had Old Faithful up my tuckus and she was telling me to inhale. My cousin Irving almost drowned in 1934. He just floated out of the bedroom.

Now at my own Seders, when we reach the portion of the service when everyone dips ten times into the wine cup to recall the ten plagues God brought down on the Egyptians, I smile to myself.

Thinking back to that terrible, wonderful Passover, I realize that if the first plague had been my mother's enema, Moses would not have had to resort to the other nine.

 ## POT ROAST

SERVES 6

The secret ingredient in this recipe is patience. To be authentic, the beef should cook very slowly for about 4 hours, just short of the point of disintegration. It should be sliceable, but almost spoonable.

The only cut to consider for this is first-cut brisket of beef. You'll want about 4 pounds. Do not, repeat, do not trim off any fat. In the immortal words of Alan King's mother, "That's the best part."

Sprinkle all sides of the meat with lots of salt and black pepper, using almost a tablespoonful of each. Place the seasoned meat in a Dutch oven and slowly begin to brown it, in its own fat, on all sides.

When fat has melted into the bottom of the pan, add 3 large onions, 3 big carrots and 3 stalks of celery, all cut in chunks, and 5 large crushed cloves of garlic. As the meat browns, so will the vegetables; they should be a medium golden brown.

When meat is seared on all sides, add about 1 inch of boiling water to the pot. Cover and let simmer slowly but steadily for 2 hours, turning meat several times. Do not pierce meat with a fork during turning; use two wooden spoons or tongs. Add more water as needed. If the heat cannot be lowered enough to keep juices simmering gently, place an asbestos pad under the pot.

After two hours, add 4 large, old boiling potatoes that have been peeled and cut in quarters. Continue cooking, turning meat and potatoes for another 2 hours, or until the meat feels very soft when pierced with a carving fork.

Half an hour before serving, carve meat into ½-inch-thick slices. Place these slices back in the gravy and keep hot over low heat for 30 minutes so that meat absorbs gravy. Remember: never skim off the fat. Alan King says that would be like taking a bath with your socks on. He has added touches to the basic recipe by using half-strength beef bouillon for the cooking instead of water.

This makes about six servings, depending, of course, on who is eating.

KARNETZLACH

SERVES 6

In a large bowl, combine 2 pounds ground beef chuck, 5 crushed garlic cloves, 1 teaspoon salt, 1 teaspoon black pepper and 1 large egg. Knead together with your hands, pressing it firmly as you do so. Gradually add ½ cup ice-cold water as you work. This will make the meat dense. When mixture is almost elastic, shape into cylinders, each a little less than 1 inch thick and about 4 inches long.

Place on a platter in a single layer. Cover with a sheet of waxed paper and chill for 24 hours. Let stand at room temperature for 30 minutes before broiling.

Broil for about 10 minutes, turning several times so all sides are brown. They may be broiled over char-

*coal or in a kitchen broiler. Put them on a plate and
stand back!*

*Serve with cold, uncooked sauerkraut, dill pickles
and pickled green tomatoes.*

CHAPTER THREE

Only Too Much

Is Enough

If there is a single refrain running through this and the preceding chapter, it is, "Wasn't it wonderful! Wasn't it terrible!" As Alan King recalled his childhood, his expression wavered between a shudder and a sigh. "How did we ever stand it?" he kept asking, half to himself. "I wouldn't have had it any other way."

Listening to the stories of his beginnings in show business, I found myself wondering where a kid of six gets the idea to be an entertainer. Those of the Freudian persuasion might conjecture that such exhibitionist behavior compensates for feelings of inadequacy or other inner miseries. To that suggestion, Alan King replies as succinctly as his Uncle Hymie, "Bullshit! With all due respects to my colleagues Woody Allen, Sid Caesar and Jonathan Winters, I must say that I never was depressed, miserable, shy or felt unloved, and I know I was never afraid of girls — not yet, at least. The only trauma I could take to an analyst is my mother's high

*colonic and somehow I just don't think that's what
made me a comedian. Anyway, I love what I have and
don't want to be cured. A kid today who is as hyper as I
was gets Valium, calms down and probably never
amounts to anything."*

*Considering his large family, however, it is possi-
ble that as its youngest member, Alan King was making
a play for attention. And because all of the other kids in
the family were geniuses, too much was expected of him
at school and so he decided to compete on his own, very
different grounds. Certainly he wanted more money
than he saw around him and the obvious role models
were the big Jewish stars of the day — Paul Muni, Al
Jolson, Jack Benny, Eddie Cantor, all of whom had a
talent not taught at school.*

W HATEVER YOU DO, DO IT WELL!"
Those were my father's parting words as he
put me aboard the Lackawanna Railroad that would
take me to my first summer job in the Catskills. I
was only fifteen, but I had already been earning
money in show business for nine years. At six, I
began singing Yiddish songs on street corners, and
the neighbors would lean out of the windows and
throw down pennies tucked into the tissue paper
that oranges used to be wrapped in. I began rehearsing at about that age, too, practicing jokes and
impersonations in front of the bedroom mirror. My
mother would walk in and catch me and then yell to
my father, "Come see what we got here. A regular
Jack Benny." She didn't like me to hang around the

house, and when I told her there was nothing else to do, she said, "I'll get you a brass band." If I kidded her, she always answered, "Save your jokes for your bums on the street. Better you should learn a trade." To that my father would answer, "Good idea! Then we'll know exactly what kind of work he's out of."

I wasn't at all scared or nervous as I sat alone on that train. I was excited and wanted to be a hit, but I did not think about being lonely or making any big social error. It all seemed like the beginning of an adventure, and that's still how I feel when I am going to some improbable-sounding faraway place. I'm always interested in seeing what will happen. That way, even the most terrible place becomes interesting.

I wasn't even scared when I was thirteen and got up on a real stage for the first time. It was a Saturday afternoon amateur show between double features at a local movie theater, and during the next three years I sang in every amateur contest in Brooklyn.

For about a year I worked at RKO Republic as a singing usher. I led the audience in following the bouncing ball under the words on the screen. My biggest hit was "Marta," the theme song of Arthur Tracy, the Street Singer, who had a Sunday morning radio program.

When I was thirteen, I managed to get on "Major Bowes' Amateur Hour." More radios in my neighborhood were tuned into that than to FDR's

Day of Infamy speech. I came in third. First prize went to the immortal Ben Sweidel, whose act consisted of hitting his bald head with the knuckle of his forefinger to accompany himself as he sang "The Bells of St. Mary's." Second prize went to a trampoline acrobat. Remember, this was radio!

There was a studio audience, of course, and it was the applause that determined the winners. With those acts ahead of me, imagine how good I must have been to come in *third*. I was dressed as a newsboy and sang "Brother, Can You Spare a Dime?"

But I got exactly what I wanted out of that — an offer to tour with a Major Bowes road company for six months at $25 a week. That was a lot of money then. The law required the company to take a tutor along for minors, but the law didn't say he had to be able to read, and this guy was illiterate. Even with a brilliant tutor my mother would have gone crazy at the idea of a thirteen-year-old leaving home and school. She couldn't understand what kind of kid she had raised, one who strayed so far from her three simple rules: Eat. Go to the bathroom. Be quiet. In that order. My father argued with her and eventually pacified her by saying, "Let him get it out of his system." When I came home for my bar mitzvah, I stayed a while and went to school.

My mother regarded my show-business ambition as a form of constipation. If she could once get it out of my system, she figured, it would be gone forever. She's still waiting.

It sure wasn't out of my system when I left for

the Catskills. I thought about all of that as the train got close to Monticello. My job was at the New Prospect Inn, which looked remarkably like the Old Prospect Inn. I kept thinking about my salary, $20 a week plus a room and all the food I could eat, which was plenty, and I hope it might also include some sex. I tried to think up some routines for my job. I was on the social staff as a porch comic, who was supposed to keep guests entertained whenever they were just sitting around. I thought up clever things, like falling in the pool with my clothes on. And for an especially big laugh, I did it when there was no water in the pool. My boss, the social director, was Phil Foster, who was just as gruff and funny then as he was on the "Laverne and Shirley" show.

I greeted him with a wisecrack, and he just looked at me, stone-cold, and made me feel at home by sounding like my mother. "Save it for the paying guests," he said. He showed me to my room, and for the first time I felt shaky. It was a tiny, narrow room in a broken-down shack, laughingly referred to as the staff's quarters. The only light came from your typical hanging bare bulb, and there were two narrow cots with mattresses that would have looked right in the set for *The Last Mile*.

The next shock came when Foster introduced me to my roommate, Lemel, a sixty-five-year-old waiter, whose first words were, "Hey, kid. Can you lend me two bucks for a sure thing?" After two days, I learned that he was an incurable horseplayer and the only sure thing was that Lemel would lose. Even though he worked in Rappaport's all winter and in the mountains all summer, he was stone-broke. The fact that our room had no closet didn't bother him at all. He was wearing everything he owned — one suit, a pair of shoes so old they looked as though he had them on sideways, one pair of socks and not even a full shirt, just a dickey with a bowtie.

The last thing I saw as I fell asleep each night and the first thing I saw in the morning was the glass of water holding Lemel's teeth standing on the rickety night table between our cots. I had the idea for *Jaws* long before Steven Spielberg. It was not exactly what a fifteen-year-old has in mind for himself his first summer away from home.

Sex was, of course, what I thought of between meals, between shows and between everything. I finally became friendly with Lemel and sort of trusted him, so one day I asked him, "What are the chances of getting laid up here?" I thought that phrasing would make me sound experienced. Foster was nearby and heard me and only afterward did I realize there was a strange glance exchanged between them.

"Say, Lemel," Foster said. "Maybe you ought to fix him up with the baker's daughter."

"The baker's daughter? Who is she?" I asked, ready even then.

"She's a nymphomaniac," Lemel answered.

In those days, that was the magic word. Not a pejorative — just a recommendation.

Foster and Lemel began to tell me about Hilda,

whose father was the baker and worked from midnight until early morning. He would have to turn out that mountain of breads, rolls, cakes, pies, cookies and Danish pastry that was consumed there every day. They said he lived in a shack in a clearing through the woods and that on the right night they would take me there.

Naturally I thought about that a lot and the rest of the staff knew I was waiting and used to drop remarks about how terrific and sexy Hilda was. Meanwhile I learned the ropes and found to my surprise that the single biggest activity up there was not swimming, tennis or handball but eating. The portions served there made my mother's look like Weight Watchers'. The guests ate to get even for everything: for people starving in Europe, for Papa who worked in the city, and with the management who was getting paid for it all anyway. When a waiter put down the breakfast menu, guests would look it over and say, "Fine! I'll have it." It was never "either/or," or "choice of." They had the whole thing. Breakfasts were wild, with all kinds of cereal and juices, eggs, blintzes, pancakes, smoked fish, cream cheese, sour cream and boiled potatoes and a dozen kinds of herring. The big favorite was the French toast, or more as it was done here, Jewish toast. It was made with thick slabs of challah that had a swollen, puffed-up, crisp outer crust. It may sound awful, but it was really delicious. I couldn't figure out how it was made, but before long I had the chance to find out.

I always woke up early when I couldn't stand
Lemel's snoring anymore. I would slip out of the
room and go into the kitchen to watch the cook, who
was the owner's sister. She would make me fendl
coffee — yesterday's coffee boiled in a saucepan
with milk. Then she beat up lots of eggs and milk to
make the French toast and added a few spoonfuls of
Aunt Jemima Pancake Mix and I realized that's
what made the fried slices so crusty and what kept
them eggy and moist inside. I still make French
toast that way.

Lunch was dairy, too, with soups, fried fish
with potatoes, vegetables and sour cream, noodles
served with pot cheese or baked in a pudding with
raisins and cinnamon, and kasha varnishkes.

"Just for a taste" was the big line. At dinner
they'd say, "All right. You'll bring me the pot roast
and then a small veal cutlet on the side. Just for a
taste." Whoever heard of a side order of veal cutlet?
Between meals there were "snecks," a little something just in case. Guests also smuggled food up to
their rooms for security. In every room there was a
salami hanging like a Calder mobile. The husbands
used to bring them up on Fridays, and I always told
a joke about the wife waiting for her husband's big
salami.

The social staff was well fed because we ate
with the guests so that we could dance with the
daughters and mingle. "Mingle" was the name of
the game. But with all of that food around, it was
hard to believe how stingy the management was to

the waiters. They were half-starved. When they went into the kitchen to ask for more food, the cook would say, "If you want lots of good food, check in. Until then, gedoudahere." By the end of the summer, we knew she was saying, "Get out of here."

Arthur Miller, the great American playwright, told me that when he was a waiter in Ellenville, he learned how to eat a lamb chop while clearing the table. When he saw a chop that had not been bitten into, he would grab it and then, in the time it took to walk from the table to the swinging door of the kitchen, he'd pick the bone clean. He'd just work it from one end to the other, as though he were playing a harmonica.

A lot of waiters stole food to sell, and Lemel did that whenever he needed money, which was always. "Hey, look at this terrific flanken," he said to anyone who would listen. By then everyone was on to him and avoided him as though he was a leper.

I suggested he ask Phil Foster for a loan. He was afraid his head would be bitten off but finally in desperation, he asked. "Loan me two dollars for two hours," he pleaded.

"Get away from me," Foster answered. "I don't wanna talk to you."

Lemel begged, "I'll give you back three dollars in two hours. The horse can't lose."

Finally Foster relented and asked what collateral Lemel had.

"I don't have anything but my false teeth," he said.

A strange glint shone in Foster's eyes. "I'll take them," he said. "You get them back when I get three dollars."

So Foster takes the teeth — uppers and lowers — and wraps them in a napkin and puts them in his pocket. Lemel is left with gums, nothing but gums.

Everybody knew about the loan and couldn't wait to see what would happen. Hours went by and still no Lemel. Finally, at four-thirty, Lemel comes back because waiters ate at five o'clock. He walks over to Foster and says, "Give me my teeth."

"Give me my three dollars," Foster demands. Lemel says the horse lost, but that he will repay the three dollars eventually.

"No, no, no," Foster says. "That's not the way it works. You don't give me three dollars, I don't give you your teeth." Then he thinks for a minute and adds, "But tell me, how much money you got on you now?"

Lemel goes through his pockets and finds a quarter. "I'll take it," Foster says, "And I'll rent you your teeth just for this meal." After Lemel ate, he washed the teeth and handed them back to Foster. And that's the way it went all summer long.

Of course that made it even more difficult than ever for Lemel to borrow money. After a few weeks, when I kept bothering him about the baker's daughter, he heaved a great sigh and said, "O.K. You give me two dollars and I'll set you up with the baker's daughter."

I agreed, but only on the condition that it take

place that night. Lemel had said that though she
didn't take any money for her services, she did love
chocolate and would be very nice to anyone who
brought her some. I bought about a five-pound
Whitman's Sampler from the concessionaire, little
realizing that Lemel got a commission on every sale.

Lemel said he would lead me to Hilda, making
sure the coast was clear. I couldn't wait for the band
to play "Good-night, Sweetheart." That was the sig-
nal because it was the end of the evening's work.

I met Lemel in the parking lot as planned, and
we began the long trek through the trees. I didn't
know, but everyone was hiding in the bushes
watching what happened. Every time I stepped on a
twig, Lemel said, "Sh! The baker might hear you."
When we got to the clearing where the cottage was,
Lemel said, "I'll go first. The baker would kill anyone who touched his daughter.

"Hilda! Hilda!" Lemel called in a stage whis-
per. "Is the coast clear?" What I did not know was
that the cottage was a toolshed and that the only
person in it was Phil Foster.

When Lemel called, Foster raised his voice in a
crazy bloodcurdling scream: "You dirty bastards!"
he shouted. "Trying to screw my daughter. I'll kill
you." With that, he smashed a light bulb onto the
floor so that it exploded and sounded like a gun shot.

"Run for your life," Lemel yelled. I thought
there was something crazy about this, but I took no
chances and ran, with chocolates flying in all directions.

When I got to the parking lot, I stopped for

breath and then the gang came out of the bushes, all laughing hysterically. Only then did they tell me that was a classic game played when some sharpie guest checked in and asked about finding action — the typical peg-pants, wide-shouldered zoot-suiter of the period. From that time on, I took over Lemel's job and led the mark to Hilda. The guy always checked out in the middle of the night.

Things got even worse for Lemel because that had been his last ploy. He had nothing left to sell. One day toward the end of the summer, he didn't have a dime and Foster wouldn't give him his teeth. By that time, Lemel had given him about ten dollars in rentals and I couldn't stand it anymore. "Phil," I said. "For God's sake, give him one free shot!" Sure enough, Foster hands them over, looking disgusted with himself for being too soft.

A few minutes later Foster walks back to the waiters' dining room and sees Lemel eating soup. Foster gets all red, his eyes glare and his fists clench. He screams, "For soup, you don't need teeth! Give 'em back!" And right in the middle of the meal, Lemel handed them over.

🌿 FRENCH TOAST

*Forget delicacy here. This is hefty, coffee-shop–
style French toast, as Alan King makes it for his family
on Sunday morning. The pancake mix is a trick used by
luncheonettes to bulk up portions, but it does add a
crisp veneer to the thick slices.*

*For each portion you will need two slices of chal-
lah, about 2 inches thick. Stale challah is best, preferably two or three days old.*

*Beat 2 large eggs into a cup of milk and when
blended, gradually stir in about 2 teaspoons of Aunt Jemima Pancake Mix and a pinch of salt. Use a whisk for
this and add the mix until you have the consistency of
very heavy cream. This batter should be made in a wide
bowl, so you can soak the slices of bread in it. Soak both
slices, turning once so they absorb the batter.*

*Meanwhile, heat about 3 tablespoons of butter in a
10-inch heavy skillet. With a slotted spatula, lift the
soaked bread out of the batter and without letting the
batter drain off place it directly into the hot butter.
Press each slice down gently with the spatula during
frying. When the first side is golden brown, about 5 to 7
minutes, turn the slice over and fry the other side,
again pressing down with the spatula.*

*Serve at once with a pat of butter on each slice and
some maple syrup or strawberry preserves on the side.
(If I'm coming to breakfast, I hope he'll have some cinnamon sugar and forget the syrup and preserves.)*

MUSHROOM AND BARLEY SOUP

MAKES ABOUT 3 QUARTS

Using a straight-sided 3- to 4-quart soup pot, place in it a 3-pound piece of first-cut beef flanken, a small marrow bone and a pinch or two of coarse salt. Add enough water to cover (about 2 to 2½ quarts). Bring to a boil.

Reduce heat. As soup simmers, skim off foam that rises to the surface. After foam has subsided and soup has simmered for 1 hour, add 2 scraped carrots, 2 stalks of celery with leaves, 1 medium-size onion, a small piece of scraped parsnip, a small piece of knob celery, and 3 or 4 sprigs of parsley.

Soak 2 large dried Polish mushroom caps in hot water for 30 minutes. Chop mushrooms and add to soup. Let sand, if any, settle in the hot water, then carefully pour soaking water into soup. After another hour, add ¼ cup washed pearl barley and ½ pound sliced fresh mushrooms. Cook for an additional hour. By that time the meat should be tender.

Discard the bone and any limp, overcooked vegetables. Dice other vegetables if necessary. Cut meat into spoon-size pieces after trimming off fat. Return to pot. Let soup stand so you can skim off fat.

CHAPTER FOUR

La Belle Simone

Listening to Alan King talk about the Riviera right after he described his first summer in the Cats-kills, I thought of calling this chapter "You've come a long way, Baby!" No wonder he felt he was in Wonder-land along the Côte d'Azur. Despite the obvious contrast of the two life-styles, he reminisced about both with much the same passion and nostalgia, as though each had contributed equally to the richness of his life.

Alan considers the best eighteen days of his life those he spent in July of 1977 aboard La Belle Simone. This fabled, gleaming white yacht was built for the mil-lionaire realtor William J. Levitt, and was named for his beautiful and gracious French wife, Simone. To get all of the details correct, I had lunch with Simone Le-vitt, who has records of dates, guests, ports of call and, above all, menus. We met at Le Cygne, where Alan joined us for a drink before going on to another date. When he left, Simone filled me in, not only with vital

*statistics on the yacht, but also with some insights on
Alan King, the Guest.*

"As guest and host, Alan is just like my husband
and many other successful men who have achieved a
lot," Simone said. "They are marvelous hosts but generally bad guests. That's because they're used to being
in charge and are uncomfortable when they are not.
They notice everything that goes wrong and figure that
they could have handled things better."

With the information from Simone Levitt and the
fine descriptions of the yacht in the book The Dream
Boats, by Nancy Holmes, I gathered some impressive
statistics. La Belle Simone was built in 1972 in Car-
rara, Italy, a location that accounts for the lavish mar-
bled bathrooms and staircase. The 225-foot boat cost $8
million to build, $1 million a year to operate, and the
annual cost for light bulbs alone was $3,200. It slept ten
and carried an international crew of between twenty-
five and thirty. When Bill Levitt sold it ten years later,
his asking price was $16 million. He sold it because
what he had first described as his "floating Taj Mahal"
turned into his "floating hotel," with all of the attendant expenses and frustrating complications.

Foremost among the crew was Chef Baldi, as well
as a Swiss pâtissier known as Little Hans and two Chinese cooks who served one meal a week complete with
chopsticks and rice bowls. Simone provided quasi-
Oriental costumes for all.

When I reported the bare statistics to Alan, he
said, "Describing La Belle Simone in terms of feet and
dollars is as futile as describing Jacqueline Bisset as
having a chemical worth of eighty-two cents. The facts
hardly give a clue to the feeling."

*Even from the photographs, it is easy to under-
stand why this shining white yacht with its slim, ta-
pering prow and sleek lines silhouetted against the blue
Mediterranean sea and sky represents to Alan King the
best of the good old days.*

I HAVE WORKED AT SO MANY RESORTS IN
my lifetime that it is almost impossible for me to
pick a place for a vacation. But whenever I can, I
head for my favorite corner of the world — the
French Riviera. When I'm in Rome, I feel like Mar-
cello Mastroianni. In Paris, I feel like Charles Boyer,
and in London, I feel like Cary Grant. But when I'm
in the south of France, I feel as though I'm going to
wake up and find myself back in the Catskills.

Not only is the landscape beautiful with the
flowers, the hills and the sea, but there is that incredible food — to me the world's best. If I had to
pick one area in which I would eat for the rest of my
life, it would be Provence. It has just the right blend
of Italian lustiness and French refinement. That
great market in Nice really says it all. That was the
first place I ever saw artichokes with their long
stems and leaves, really looking like thistles. And
the incredible colors of the tomatoes, the eggplants
and the peppers!

Whenever I'm there I have a slice of pissala-
dière, the great Nice pizza with the soft onions and
the oil and little black olives. Once Jeanette and I
took a quick last walk through that market just be-

fore we were to catch a plane. I was wearing a blazer and white slacks, and I couldn't resist having a pan bagna, that sandwich on a big round French roll that is slathered with olive oil and layered with tomatoes, onions, peppers and anchovies.

"Look at yourself," Jeanette suddenly yelled. "You're full of food stains."

Looking down at the tomatoes and oil that had dripped all over me, I answered, "Yeah, but they are the food stains of Provence — badges of honor!"

In the early fifties, when Jeanette and I went to the Riviera, we stayed at small *pensions* and we would walk around the Cannes harbor envying owners of the fantastic yachts anchored there. We wondered what life aboard one would be like. It took us about twenty years, but we finally found out on several trips aboard *La Belle Simone.* It was even more fabulous than our daydreams. The most memorable trip — the one that stands for them all — lasted for eighteen days. Other guests were Sue and Herman Merinoff; John Mills, the owner of and gracious host at the London club Les Ambassadeurs, and his wife, Diane; and Susan and John Weitz, the designer.

Simone and Bill are great hosts, and on that trip, their hospitality began when our plane landed at Nice. They sent a car with two crewmen to pick us up and clear our luggage through customs. The yacht's colors were brown and tan and so were the crewmen's shirts and even the Rolls-Royce was brown. They drove us to Monte Carlo, where the boat was anchored. Once aboard, our luggage was whisked away and unpacked. Remembering that would happen, I made sure to buy new underwear and the kosher salami I always carry as a security blanket was stashed in my hand luggage.

The interior of the ship was magnificent. The main salon and dining room looked like Versailles done up in Louis-the-Something. There was a charming lounge, the Café du Ciel, on the upper aft deck that could be reached by elevator. Bill Levitt is an accomplished pianist, and he had a white piano in the Café and another of walnut in the main salon. Each bedroom looked like the royal suite at the Paris Ritz. There was a terry robe by Givenchy for every guest, and bathrooms were complete with cosmetics, toiletries, shaving accessories and anything else you could think of. There was no need for a sewing kit because there was a seamstress on board.

Best of all for me, there were practically no rules. We could have breakfast anywhere or not at all. We could swim in the pool with or without the Jacuzzi, or play backgammon with Bill, or, if we felt up to it, we could take on Simone, a world-class hand wrestler.

Lunches were gorgeous. Before the food there were Bellinis — champagne with peaches as invented at Harry's Bar in Venice. The lunch buffet would include oeufs en gelée, crudités, and a rainbow salad of all different colored shredded vegetables arranged in stripes. There might be hot crepes filled with crabmeat or cold shrimp and langoustine and always a fish that had been caught that morning and then grilled or poached. Little Hans made fresh rolls every day, as well as great desserts, such as kiwi or mango ice cream and crisp butter cookies. Hans was a genius and famous for the special cakes he created for celebrity guests. For Rex Harrison, he made a big flowered picture-hat cake, like those worn by ladies at the Ascot races. For Roger Moore, he baked and frosted an almost life-size saint. And for Gregory Peck, it was a great white whale. For me,. his offering was a coffee cake — a giant Russian Jewish babka. Was he trying to tell me something?

We all met for the start of the voyage in Monte Carlo because we had been invited to a big Red Cross Gala sponsored by Princess Grace and Prince Rainier. Before going to the party, we had drinks aboard. When we left *La Belle Simone,* she sailed a little way out in the harbor and dropped anchor just opposite the terrace of the summer casino where the ball was being held. From there, we could see the yacht's necklace of colored lights, looking like something in the Tivoli Gardens in Copenhagen.

At two in the morning, when the Gala ended, a launch took us to the yacht. Magnums of Dom Pérignon were cooling in buckets, just as they always were on that boat. The minute the last guest was aboard, the boat set sail. We stood on the bow in the summer's night breeze, with the music and lights of Monte Carlo fading in the distance.

The next morning we awoke to find ourselves

in Saint-Tropez. I had a slight hangover, my throat was dry and I sounded hoarse, so the bartender suggested a Sazerac, saying it was a better cure than orange juice. "Don't mind if I do," I answered, coining the phrase that was to be my motto throughout the trip. Then Simone and Bill revealed the itinerary. From Saint-Tropez we would go to Majorca, then to Gibraltar and Marbella, then across the Mediterranean to Sardinia and through the Straits of Messina. Next it would be the Greek Islands, the Dalmatian Coast of Yugoslavia and finally Venice, after which Jeanette and I would fly to Rome and back to New York and reality.

After breakfast, Chef Baldi came on deck and made an announcement. "Ladies and gentlemen," he said, "on the last night of this voyage, in Venice, there will be a special dinner. Each of you may select a favorite dish that I will prepare for that meal. I must know your choice three days in advance so I can buy the ingredients and I ask that you keep your choices secret so the meal will have surprises. Meanwhile, throughout the voyage, I will prepare my specialties so that you can choose from them. Or if you prefer, I will make any dish you name."

My mind was already spinning with possibilities as we went ashore that day in Saint-Tropez. Sometimes we had lunch or dinner in port to give the chef a rest or if there was some special restaurant we wanted to try. That day we had lunch at Lei Mouscardins, a café-restaurant in the harbor, closed in with sunny yellow canvas awnings. For starters, I

ordered the moules marinières and said I would see
what I felt like after that. I have never had them that
good before or since — just the sweet, shiny, black
mussels in a perfect garlic, shallot and white wine
broth glistening with flecks of butter. When the
waiter asked what I wanted for the second course, I
said, "How about some moules marinières?" When
he took the dessert orders, he said to me, "And I
suppose Monsieur would like moules marinières?"
"Don't mind if I do," I answered and I did.

But back on the boat that night for dinner, we
had an unbelievable duck pâté with just a touch of
Cognac and garlic, and I began to think of ordering
that for the dinner instead of the mussels. Then
came gambas à la plancha — shrimp baked in their
shells in a salt crust. After that there were medal-
lions of veal sautéed with prosciutto and melted
Gruyère on top, and for dessert, homemade currant
ice cream. Obviously this would be difficult. How
could I choose? And this was only the first day. I
began to nudge Jeanette, telling her to let me order
for her because she wouldn't eat anyway. That way,
I could have two choices. I even thought of buying
the rights to choose from the others on board.

My mind was churning with food ideas during
two otherwise restful days in Majorca, but gradually
I was getting excited about something else — the
sight of Gibraltar from the sea. Our captain, Klaus
Gotsch, said it would come into view at 5:30 A.M. I
awoke just in time and to prove I could still rough it
I made my own Sazerac and went onto the bridge.

Slowly the rock loomed up, looking ghostly through the mist and fog. It's truly one of the world's great symbols, and I was so impressed that I considered switching all of my insurance to Prudential.

Gibraltar is a duty-free port and Bill Levitt wanted to stop there to replace his stock of Dom Pérignon and liquor. John Mills and I wanted to load up on Cuban cigars. We walked into Shalimar, one of the duty-free shops, which was run by Ravi, a young Indian. The women headed for the jewelry, the perfumes, the scarves and handbags. Men went for pipes, watches, cigarette lighters, brandy and ties. I spotted pre-Castro cigars in the glass-fronted humidor and I asked for a dozen boxes. John Mills ordered the same. But Ravi gave us one of those little smiles and rolled his head back and forth and around. We thought he was saying yes, but the words came out, "No. We sell only one box with each purchase of other merchandise."

"Stop everything!" John and I yelled to Bill and the women. "When you check out what you bought, separate the lot into single purchases." And so it went — one bottle of Arpège, one box of Cuban cigars. Another bottle of Arpège, another box of Cuban cigars. One necktie, a box of cigars, a second tie and another box of cigars. Seeing that we were determined and that this could take some time, thereby backing up all of the other shoppers in the store, Ravi relented. "All right, all right," he finally said, his eyes downcast in defeat. Feeling sorry for him, I said, "Let that be a lesson. Never fool around with a kid who learned his shopping techniques around the pushcarts of Orchard Street."

My mind was brought back to food and my delicious dilemma that day at lunch aboard *La Belle Simone*. It began with oeufs en cocotte, baked in little ramekins lined with melted cheese, which you stirred into the yolk of the egg. There was salmon caviar rolled into cornets of smoked Scotch salmon and pressed, grilled chicken diavolo, crunchy with spicy mustard crumbs. There were also meatballs and sausages with spaghetti.

Herman Merinoff had some and pronounced it "Sensational."

I thought so too, so I said, "Why don't you order that for the big dinner?"

"What's it to you?" he asked. "Mind your own business!"

So I tried my persuasive tactics on Jeanette with no more success. Maybe I could convince her to order several desserts, I thought. Then we could have the apricot feuilleté that Little Hans sometimes served warm for breakfast, or the crepes suzette he made better than anyone else.

The next port was Marbella, with its pretty little cafés around the harbor of Puerto Banus. It was a delight to be greeted by one of the friendly natives — Stewart Granger, who looked as dashing as he did in *Beau Brummel*. By way of welcome, he had arranged a dinner for us at his favorite local restaurant. I was dressed and beginning to have cocktails at seven, forgetting that in Spain dinner starts at ten. By the time others gathered at nine, I had

had a two-hour head start, just the handicap I usually give my friends. Nevertheless, Merinoff, Mills, Weitz and Levitt — black-belt drinkers, all — caught up with me. Having had a small problem navigating as we walked off the gangplank, I was happy to hear Granger suggest we rest for a moment at a nice bar he knew along the way.

By the time we got to the restaurant, we were all starved and really dug into those tapas, the little appetizers they do in Spain. There were sausages in an oily paprika sauce, red peppers with garlic, chicken livers in meat sauce and snails in hot sauce. The food sobered me up a bit, a condition I immediately corrected by downing a bottle of chilled red rioja. Just after that, the snails began screaming to get out of the hot sauce and I knew it was time for me to excuse myself and make a beeline for the boat.

Somehow I found *La Belle Simone* and our cabin. I knew I was really drunk when I was lying on the floor and had to hold on. I fell asleep for an hour and when I woke up, I didn't feel bad at all, except for a dry throat. After a Sazerac, a shower and a change of clothes, I felt fine and headed back to the restaurant. By that time, everyone else was drunk and even Jeanette had a buzz on. Bill Levitt was playing the piano. Jeanette was doing a flamenco with John Mills, and Simone was singing "Lady of Spain" with the Los Paraguyas trio. I took one long, cool look around and announced, "If there's one thing I hate, it's being with drunks." And I left.

In the morning, everyone felt like hell and

wanted to sleep late. But promptly at eight I begin to
hear Latin singing and guitars. "Shut off the goddam Muzak!" I yelled. Then I realized the sound
was coming from the other side of my door. I opened
it and there were Los Paraguyas, serenading me.
The night before, Mills had arranged for them to
come aboard and awaken us with a Latin reveille.

The partying continued until lunch and I decided that one only thing worthy of such festivities
was my kosher salami, which I had been saving for a
rainy day. I took it to Chef Baldi and tried to explain
how to make salami and eggs. He tried it once but
wasn't getting it. He sliced the meat too thin and
proceeded as for a French omelet. At last I took over
and made one. When I flipped it over to brown the
second side, he jumped away from me and cried,
"Why didn't you say so, Mr. King? It's a frittata!"
It smelled so good that everyone had the same
thing.

As I started to eat mine, I said, "Now if only we
had a bialy . . ."

"We do," answered Bill Levitt as he went into
the freezer to get his security-blanket cache of
bagels and bialys.

After that, we had two more days of exquisite
eating as we sailed to Porto Cervo on the Costa
Smeralda of Sardinia. For lunch we went to a flowery terrace restaurant with a lavish buffet. I took
one look at all of the beautiful food and I realized
that I wanted something simple and familiar. I
asked the maître d' if by any chance he had chopped
vegetables with pot cheese and sour cream, the way

my mother used to make. As he was obviously puzzled, I described the dish in detail and he said, "I think we can come close, Monsieur." Next thing I knew, a captain and a waiter were at my side with a rolling table and they began mincing cucumbers, radishes, scallions, red and green peppers and watercress. The captain rubbed a big white porcelain soup bowl with a cut clove of garlic and coarse salt and he turned the vegetables into that. They put it in front of me with side dishes of ricotta and crème fraîche. I mixed it all together and as a final flourish, the captain ground some black pepper on top.

They made such a ceremony out of the whole thing that everyone in the dining room was staring. Just then, the young Aga Khan entered the room and came over to greet the Levitts. Seeing the scene around me, he asked, "May I ask what it is you are eating?"

With Jeanette kicking me under the table, I said, "Oh, it's just salade à la façon de ma mère."

Within twenty minutes, five other tables ordered what seemed the new "in" dish. I didn't have the heart to tell them it really should be eaten with dark Russian pumpernickel. Besides, if I had mentioned it, Bill Levitt might have run back to the boat to get some from his freezer.

As we sailed around the Greek islands and along the coast of Yugoslavia, I was still trying to decide between paella, bouillabaisse, and my old favorite, pot-au-feu. Our great meal was getting close.

While we were in Dubrovnik, Jeanette exchanged some money in a bank and forgot her passport. We found that out the hard way. As we were crossing the Adriatic toward Venice, we were boarded by an armed Yugoslav coastal patrol. They wanted to see the ship's manifests and all papers and passports. Jeanette dug into her purse, searched the room and then realized her passport was missing. After heavy diplomatic negotiations, aided by donations of two cases of Haig & Haig Pinch and six boxes of my Cuban cigars, we were allowed to continue.

As soon as we docked in Venice's Grand Canal, we had to get Jeanette a passport so we could leave for home. To our surprise, we discovered that the nearest consulate was in Trieste. We hired a car and driver, and the Merinoffs, loyal friends that they are, volunteered to come with us, probably to keep me from killing Jeanette. Our chauffeur must have driven the getaway car for Al Capone, but we finally arrived in Trieste, shaken but in one piece. The consulate was a group of tiny rooms on the fourth floor of an office building. By the time we found it, they were hanging out the Closed for Lunch sign. We decided we might as well have lunch, too. I asked our driver if he knew of a good restaurant, "Oh, si, Boss!" he answered. "I am from Trieste."

He took us to a small, antique trattoria called Suban. I took one look at the dark, deserted bar and figured, "Oh, no! Not me!" But as we walked into the large bright dining room and saw a big open kitchen full of copper pans and cooks dashing around, I felt more hopeful. There were pictures of chefs on the walls and a big painting of a guy who looked like Il Duce. I recognized him as the chef in the kitchen, even though he wore formal clothes in the picture and had on whites now.

He looked at me, thought for a moment, then said, "I know you from the televish. I seen you when I visited my brother in Pittsburgh. You on the Eddy O'Sullivan show!"

I looked around and saw what seemed like a huge tank full of all kinds of marvelous shining fish. From that, the chef chose things for a fabulous zuppa de pesce to which he added squid, clams, mussels and langoustine. The broth had tomatoes, garlic, white wine and parsley and he spooned it over very thin spaghetti. While we waited for the soup he served us little dishes of olives, slices of fresh mozzarella, slivered roasted peppers and a few slices of pale pink prosciutto. I don't know how many bottles of cold white wine we drank. For dessert, he brought ripe figs, peaches, and grapes in big bowls of ice water. We sat there eating from twelve-thirty to four and almost forgot the consulate. We made a mad dash for it and got there just in time.

The next day we strolled around the Piazza San Marco and sat at the cafés listening to twelve string quartets play different tunes at the same time and we took a boat ride to the Lido. Everyone was trying to remain cool and nonchalant and no one spoke about the big meal to come, nor did anyone give his or her choices away.

Finally the hour came. We met back on the

yacht in the Café du Ciel for drinks. The women looked beautiful in the caftans and jewelry they had bought as we traveled and the men wore black tie. Although we all tried to act nonchalant, everyone was distracted, wondering what the menu would be.

The suspense mounted as we entered the dining room and the secret choices gradually were revealed. The meal began with caviar and scrambled eggs in egg shells, the choice of Susan Weitz. Then came Herman Merinoff's dish, langoustines à la Belle Simone, broiled in their shells and topped with beurre fondu, then flambéed with Cognac. But who would believe that Jeanette's choice was gazpacho! Whether you consider it a wet salad or a cold soup, it's like eating nothing.

Main courses followed. Sue Merinoff had paella. John Weitz opted for bouillabaisse. Bill Levitt stuck to his favorite meatballs, sausages and spaghetti. As each dish appeared, looking marvelous, I wondered if I had made a mistake. But one glimpse of my platter and I knew I had chosen correctly — pot-au-feu, which the chef made with a moist and tender capon, succulent beef, coteghino sausage, surrounded by bright, firm carrots, celery and leeks. He served it with a hot, pungent horseradish cream sauce. John Mills, born in Warsaw, went Polish on us and had Pojarski cutlets, made of ground veal and chicken breast and fried in a thin, golden breading. Thin, crisp slices of fried eggplant was Simone's selection. Although we each ate our own main course, there was plenty of tasting back and forth. I had my wish for dessert: there were several, including apricot tart, crepes, a baked Alaska and an incredible dark, bittersweet-chocolate mousse.

Jeanette and I woke up the next morning saddened to realize this floating fantasy had come to an end. As our plane flew over Venice, we looked down at the gold and bronze rooftops, the pink palaces, the winding canals and saw the white form of *La Belle Simone*. There were tears in our eyes. I squeezed Jeanette's hand and said, "Not bad for two kids from Williamsburg. For eighteen days we were aboard a beautiful yacht and we ate the most glorious foods of France, Spain and Italy."

"Not so fast," said Jeanette. "Let me remind you that the three meals you were most excited about were salami and eggs, vegetables with pot cheese and boiled flanken with horseradish sauce."

You know something? She was right. I had not come quite so far as I thought.

 POT-AU-FEU

SERVES 8 TO 10

Place a 3-pound piece of first-cut brisket or beef rump in a 7-quart soup pot along with a 5- to 6-pound capon and a 3-pound piece of veal rump. Cover with about 4 quarts beef and / or chicken stock or cold water. Bring to a boil, reduce heat and simmer half-covered, skimming foam from surface as it rises.

When foam subsides, add 2 teaspoons coarse salt

and about 10 black peppercorns. Simmer gently but steadily, half-covered, for 1 hour.

Add 3 scraped carrots, 1 small white turnip, 2 medium-sized washed leeks, 1 large onion studded with 3 cloves, 2 cloves unpeeled garlic, 4 stalks of celery with leaves, 3 or 4 sprigs of parsley, a pinch of thyme and 1 bay leaf. Continue simmering, adding more hot liquid if the meat and chicken are not well covered. Simmer for 2 more hours, or until meat and chicken are tender.

The coteghino sausage (purchased at an Italian delicatessen or butcher's) is best cooked separately so the broth does not get greasy. Poach it in water to cover for 1 hour, while the pot-au-feu is simmering. Remove and add to pot-au-feu, simmering all for another 30 minutes.

Remove meat and vegetables and reserve. Strain broth and skim off grease. Discard any vegetables that are overcooked. If you like, cook a few fresh ones in a small amount of the broth. Serve soup as a first course, adding some rice or vermicelli. Serve meats and chicken sliced, with vegetables. Boiled potatoes and cabbage can be added to the assortment. Pass horseradish sauce separately.

 ## HORSERADISH SAUCE

To 2 cups medium-thick béchamel sauce, add 2 to 3 tablespoons freshly grated horseradish. Season with white pepper and lemon juice. If you use bottled horseradish, add the same amount but drain it well and eliminate lemon juice.

FRIED EGGPLANT IN BEER BATTER

SERVES 6 TO 8

Select two very ripe (black-skinned) eggplants of medium size. Peel and cut in half lengthwise, then cut into slices just a little more than ¼-inch thick.

To prepare batter, stir together 2 cups sifted flour, a pinch of salt, 1 tablespoon olive or vegetable oil, 1 egg yolk, ¾ cup unchilled beer and ¼ cup warm water. Stir smooth with a wire whisk. Just before dipping the eggplant slices into batter, fold in 2 stiffly beaten egg whites.

Dip each slice in batter. Let excess drip off, then deep-fry in vegetable oil that is 375 degrees on a fat thermometer. Fry two slices at a time. Frying time for each batch should be about 7 minutes. Turn so that both sides of the slices become golden brown. Drain for a minute or two on paper towel, then place on a rack in an open baking pan.

Heat all slices in a 350-degree oven for about 7 or 8 minutes, or until fat drains off and batter is crisp. Serve immediately with salt and lemon juice. Do not salt eggplant before it is fried or it will become soggy.

CHAPTER FIVE

Feeders, Fanatics and Feinschmeckers

Through the years, Alan King has developed a list not only of memorable meals, but also of equally memorable eaters, some great, others crazy. "Eating takes a special talent," he says. "Some people are much better at it than others. In that way, it's like sex, and as with sex, it's more fun with someone who really likes it. I can't imagine having a lasting friendship with anyone who is not interested in food."

Despite that feeling, Alan King has managed to sustain a marriage to a woman whose diet seems to consist of raw vegetables and cookies. But in truth, Jeanette King is interested in food, if only negatively. In an effort to avoid calories, she probably thinks about it as much as her husband.

This is as good a place as any to describe Alan King as an eater, great or crazy. After sharing many meals with him, and even more conversations about food, I would say he is much closer to greatness than to crazi-

ness, although he does have some limiting idiosyncrasies. He spends a great deal of time, money and effort to learn about those foods that interest him, finding out just how they should be prepared and tracking down recommended products. This may include such items as Italian sausages flown in to Aspen for a dinner he is cooking, or a loaf of brioche, which is akin to challah, as the perfect base for his French toast. Planning meals is among his top half-dozen passions, whether it is his own dinner to be decided upon before he gets out of bed in the morning, a party at his home for friends or what he will order a week from next Sunday at Chasen's in Los Angeles, at Bacigalup's in Flushing during the U.S. Open or at La Grenouille in Manhattan. A man who takes all sorts of risks in business and at the gambling tables, Alan King will not leave any of his personal comforts to chance. "There's no pot luck in my personal life" is the way he puts it.

But that reluctance to take risks limits him somewhat from experimentation. He rarely orders fish, other than lobster, as a main course for dinner. He has never said, "Let's go to a Japanese restaurant" — thereby wiping out at least some dishes he would probably like. What seems to worry Alan King the most in eating (and perhaps in life) is the wasted opportunity, the notion that in the interest of experimentation he might lose the chance to enjoy the known condition that pleases him.

What he has no patience with is a meal of small sample tastings, in the manner of the menu de dégustation. *He would rather have two or three substantial courses. Perhaps the tasting menu seems to be a teaser, gastronomic foreplay that never quite gets to the main event. Alan King also hates to taste other people's food or to give them tastes of his. "Taste it," friends tell him when they have ordered something different. "What they really want is a taste of mine," he says, "and they don't get it." He takes pride in the practice of many friends who, when dining with him in a restaurant, wait to hear what he orders and then follow suit. "My good friend Stephen Levy for twenty years has examined menus and asked for descriptions of dishes and then says, 'I'll have what Mr. King is having.' "*

Despite his reluctance to try new dishes, when he is confronted with one that is well prepared and stylish, he is quick to recognize it and adopt it. At our first lunch at Il Nido, the proprietor, Adi Giovannetti, prepared a surprise dessert he knew I had liked in Milan. It was simplicity itself, a platter of sliced, peeled ripe pears alternating with chunks of well-aged Parmesan cheese and shelled walnut meats. Whenever he knew friends were going to Il Nido, Alan King called the restaurant and ordered that dessert for them, asking that it be charged to him.

A lusty eater who likes substantial food, Alan King hates gargantuan portions that make him feel stuffed. But it is likely that he could eat several meals a day and if left to his own devices could weigh as much as Orson Welles, who, he says, once devoured a whole country.

LIVING WITH JEANETTE, I'VE TAKEN A postgraduate course in crazy eaters. I really learned to cook in self-defense. For the first twenty-six dinners of our married life, she broiled lamb chops. I suggested that since she was so good at broiling, she apply that skill to chicken and steak.

But no, on the twenty-seventh night it was lamb chops again and I said, "O.K. That's it! I'm taking over." For the next ten years I not only couldn't eat the meat of a lamb but I even became allergic to the wool from its back. I've been doing the cooking ever since.

But Jeanette came by it honestly. Her mother, who was a lovely woman in all other ways, was the world's worst cook. She invented health food and nouvelle cuisine before anyone else ever thought about them. Nothing had salt, pepper or any other seasoning, and she always mashed the food so that it looked as though it had already been eaten.

Her rule was that if it tasted good, it couldn't be healthful. One of her diets almost became an international incident. In 1970 I went to the ground-breaking ceremonies of the Alan King Diagnostic Medical Center in Ramat Eshkol in Israel. I took about thirty people with me, including my family and friends such as Barbara Walters, Simone and Bill Levitt and Josephine Baker. During the ceremonies, I was on the dais next to a Druse sheikh who invited me and all of my guests to his village.

We piled into a bus on the appointed day and as we were driving over, the guide told us what a rare honor such an invitation was. The whole scene was out of *Beau Geste* — the men with long beards and white caftans, the women who had to stay out of sight and who peeked through pierced screens, the costumed children who danced for us, and the big table in the courtyard piled with those sticky honey

pastries that are so sweet you get diabetes just looking at them. The Druse do not drink alcohol, so
there were many toasts drunk in orange soda. Men
in that society have very little to do with women, but
out of courtesy the sheikh tried to emulate Western
ways and he approached my mother-in-law, offering
a tray of those pastries. He could not speak English.
He just held out the tray. She took one look and said,
"Danks, Your Majesty. But I'm on a salt-free diet."

Jeanette is a lot like her. I'll never forget our
fifth anniversary, when I wanted to buy her a $5,000
diamond ring. I was broke and in Las Vegas, so I
went to the crap table to try and win the money. Instead I lost $25,000, which I didn't have and which
it took me three years to repay. Joe E. Lewis, my
mentor, offered to lend me the $5,000, saying I
should just pretend I had lost $30,000. I took it and
bought the ring and he planned an anniversary
party at Chasen's for the event. A lot of our friends
were there, including Red Skelton, Danny Thomas
and Joan Crawford, and many other Hollywood celebrities were around the room.

The ring was in a tiny box and Dave Chasen,
who was a sweet little man, wrapped it in waxed
paper and had the baker put it in one of the small individual tarts he was preparing and top it off with
whipped cream. We figured Jeanette would cut into
her tart and find the ring. Everyone else knew about
the surprise and was watching our table. When the
pastry tray was passed around, damned if Jeanette
didn't announce that she didn't want dessert. "I'm

too full," she kept saying. I told her the tarts were made especially for us and she had to have one. But she just kept shaking her head and saying no. Finally, I lost my temper and told her that if she didn't take at least one bite, I would stab her in the arm with my fork. Neither of us is sure to this day whether I meant it. Then she cut the tart, found the ring and got all excited. Everyone in the room cheered. She still gets full from food, but she never gets fed up with diamonds.

The few times when Jeanette did experiment with food have been disasters. During one trip to Madrid, she ate fried squid and thought it was wonderful french fries. When I told her what it was, she got sick and didn't eat anything for three days. Then we went to El Botín, the place that makes the great suckling pigs, and just her luck — she got the squiggly tail. That was all she needed to make her go on another three-day fast. I figured she was squeamish, but I was wrong. On the following day we went to a bull fight and when the dashing toreador handed her the prize ear, she jumped up and down with joy.

Our daughter, Elainie, is a third-generation weird eater. She's as changeable as the weather in Chicago. One day she's a vegetarian, the next she's on a bacon diet and in between, she's also a closet Oreo eater. Once I made ziti with sausages for a whole gang of friends and made separate sauce for her. She made me swear there was no meat in her portion. I thought I'd have to take an oath on a bible.

Our two sons eat more like me. Robert, the older, considers my tastes lowbrow, especially when I cook with College Inn broth. My other son, Andy, eats everything as long as he can smell it first. He really sniffs at all his food and so does his son, Teddy. I can tell what he eats by examining the tip of his nose.

But theirs are small idiosyncrasies compared to some of the wild eaters I have known, several of whom carried special ingredients around in silver cases. Zubin Mehta, who naturally was raised on Indian food, likes hot spices and carries fiery chili peppers in a silver snuff box. Even if he is at a restaurant like Lutèce, he pulls the box out when no one is looking and sprinkles the peppers onto his food. His wife, Nancy, once ordered a special dinner for us at the Raga restaurant and it included a fish flown in from India that was so hotly seasoned I had to have a side order of Nupercainal for the blisters on my lips.

Joan Crawford was another carrier, but her specialty was Russian vodka in an antique flask. Her other specialty was throwing up after every meal. Carol Channing carries organic vegetarian food in a silver container wherever she goes, and Woody Allen, who is serious about food, carries a bottle of Lafite-Rothschild 1969 to every restaurant. He even takes it to Rao's in Spanish Harlem. Now that's my kind of wino.

The Kennedys specialized in simplicity when it came to meals. I have eaten at Hyannisport, at

McLean, Virginia, and at several of their other homes and the food was always of the best quality, carefully cooked, but very simple — clam chowder, corn, steaks, lobsters and lots of roast beef. They also did a lot of outdoor cooking. Steve Smith makes the best daiquiris I've ever had. One of Jack Kennedy's big favorites was bean soup, either in the Senate dining room or at Bookbinder's in Philadelphia, where he always ordered it for the Army-Navy game.

I have also known eaters who specialize in a particular dish. Danny Thomas, who also smells food before he eats it and whose nose makes it possible for him to sniff the food across the room, is a bologna sandwich maven. He likes them on hamburger rolls and eats them three times a day. But he never trusts a kitchen to make one right. Even at the Bistro Garden in Beverly Hills it takes him ten minutes to order. He explains that the bologna must be hand-sliced and a quarter-inch thick. There has to be iceberg lettuce and unsalted butter on both cut sides of the roll and he does not like the finished sandwich to be cut in half.

Once I couldn't take it anymore and I yelled, "Enough already with the bologna sandwich."

"Alan, what do you know about ecstasy?" he answered.

Lebanon is famous for its food, but a bologna sandwich is not the national dish.

Another specialist was Walter Hyman, a wonderful guy who was my partner in many Broadway productions. He was a great, generous friend. If you went window-shopping with him, he would buy you two windows. All he ever ate was a tongue sandwich at Schrafft's, followed by an Orange Julius on Broadway — the world's most bizarre progressive dinner. Many a night he would have guests at the Colony and he'd say he had to check on the box office.

Then he'd get the sandwich and the drink and come back, saying he was not hungry. One year Walter went to Europe, dieted and lost twenty-five pounds. He also got a toupee. When he got back, he asked me to meet him for lunch at "21" and as soon as we met, he asked, "How do I look?" Being a good friend, I answered, "Like a guy who lost twenty-five pounds and bought a toupee." With that, Walter ripped the toupee off in disgust, right at the table.

Sidney Lumet, the director, also specializes. He only eats take-out Chinese food from paper containers. He's so used to having it that way that even when he's in a Chinese restaurant he asks to have it served in containers.

And this may come as a big surprise — Frank Sinatra is Italian, never more so than when he eats. What he really likes is the paterfamilias role and he loves a lot of friends around the table. Sinatra alone is twenty people. He's always in charge and knows what everyone should have and orders it — like a Jewish mother. "It's good for you," he says if anyone should object. He's branching out lately and his tastes are getting sophisticated. Now when he is in New York he alternates between the excellent Neapolitan food at Patsy's and the elegant French food at La Grenouille. Not long ago he was at that beautiful restaurant with Henry Kissinger and I was seated on the banquette next to Sinatra, although I was with other people. He kept passing me caviar canapés under the tablecloth. After the fourth or fifth I whispered, "Frank, that's enough." He said, "Eat it. It's good for you."

Frank's big cooking specialty is spaghetti sauce and once I was a guest at his home in Palm Springs and walked into the kitchen while he was cooking. Damned if he wasn't working behind a sort of screen he had erected with tablecloths stretched across a clothesline.

We once got into an argument about the best way to make sauce. Frank's buddy, Jilly Rizzo, was there and so was The Hook — his bodyguard. The argument got heated and suddenly Frank jumped up, pointed at me and yelled, "Why are we listening to him? What does a Jew know about making spaghetti sauce!" Frank's recipe for tomato sauce was a better-kept secret than the formula for Coca-Cola syrup, but you'll find it at the end of this chapter.

I've known a lot of amazing big eaters. Before his diet Sid Caesar could eat a chair, with its footstool. Buddy Hackett eats everything but the kitchen sink. That he has with a glass of milk before going to bed. Imagine being on a rice diet and smelling pizza in your sleep? That's how Hackett got to be persona non grata at the reducing clinic at Duke University. He used to go for the rice diet, then slip pieces of pizza under the doors of other patients at night. He has more recently been expelled by Pritikin for similar pranks.

Not all big eaters are discerning, of course, but Orson Welles is both and I guess one of the four most memorable eaters I have known. Compared with Orson, Diamond Jim Brady was on a crash diet. But Orson really knows what he is eating. He once took me to Chez Denis in Paris and ordered a fantastic meal. I can still remember the tastes of sweetbreads with truffles, the lobster bordelaise and the incredible fillet of beef topped with a thick slice of foie gras. Watching Orson Welles eat is like watching a sex orgy. It's a real turn-on. The meals I shared with him are among the greatest joys of my life, not only because he knows food, but because he is such a brilliant conversationalist. Good talk at meals is almost as important as good food.

We ate together for a whole week in New York when we were working on a project, and we went to all kinds of restaurants — French, Italian, Russian. Orson was dressed in black and looked like a stolen car. In each restaurant he spoke the language. But when I took him to the Yun Luck Rice Shoppe in Chinatown and he ordered in Chinese, that was too much.

"Listen, Orson! I've had it with you," I told him.

He brushed it off, saying, "Nothing to it. I picked it up while traveling with my father, who was a newspaperman in China for many years."

Edward G. Robinson was a connoisseur of everything — clothing, art, cigars and food. We once had dinner at Henri Soulé's Pavillon and what made the meal memorable was not only the fabulous food, but the conversation we carried on in mama-lushen, a down-home Yiddish dialect. He spoke it meticulously and the waiters were staring, wondering what language it was.

John Huston is another great companion at meals. He's a big man in every way — size, stature, talent and eating ability. We made the film *Lovesick,* starring little Dudley Moore. The three of us would go to lunch together and Huston and I would have three good-sized courses while Dudley nibbled on a raw carrot. Huston kept staring at him through his deep-set eyes, rubbing his grizzly beard thoughtfully. Finally he asked slowly and deliberately, "Dudley, do you eat that way because you're small or are you small because you eat that way?"

John Huston was a four-pack-a-day smoker but developed emphysema and had to stop. Not wanting to torment him during that lunch, I jumped up every five minutes to go to the men's room for a cigarette. As I got up for the fourth trip, John asked me if I was having bladder problems. When I told him why I was leaving the table, he said, "Please. Smoke in front of me and *please* blow the smoke in my face." What a considerate man! Nonsmokers, please note.

Of the four, I suppose the biggest and craziest eater was Zero Mostel. He was also the most delicious man I ever knew. We once had a meal that lasted for six hours. It was at the old Parkway restaurant on the Lower East Side. It went from chopped chicken livers, through stuffed cabbage, two kinds of soup, boiled beef, to pot roast with chopped garlic and a steak so big it hung over the plate. With most people it's steak *or* chops. With Zero it was steak *and* chops. And all the potatoes — not just the silver dollars but the pancakes, the mashed with onions and the boiled. He must have eaten five loaves of challah plus matzo and I don't know how much chicken fat he poured over his food from the pitcher on the table. I do know he poured a lot of it into his jacket pocket. "It's to go with the grated radish I put there a few minutes ago," he explained to the awe-struck diners at the next table.

But maybe the really craziest eater I know is Mickey Hayes, the unofficial mayor of Miami Beach, who owns a haberdashery there. The only things he would eat were Moosebeck sardines (which he calls Moose-ah-beck), Vita chopped herring, Bumble Bee salmon and, for a beverage, egg creams made with Fox's U-Bet chocolate syrup.

Mickey hated mayonnaise more than anything in the world. He couldn't be at the same table with anyone eating it, even if it was in a sandwich. In 1962 Mickey bought his first Cadillac, a big convertible. Jack Carter was visiting him and when the car was delivered, Mickey was not home. Carter called me to come over. He had a great idea. We went to Mickey's parked car with a jar of Hellmann's mayonnaise and rubbed it all over the steering wheel. Mickey arrived and took one look and knew immediately what was on the wheel. Without ever getting into the car, he called the dealer to come and

pick it up. He took a $600 loss on a car that didn't
have two miles on it. Now that's what I call a dislike
for mayonnaise.

I once caught my wife cheating with Mickey.
Now, hold on! It was not that kind of cheating! We
were staying at the Hôtel du Cap on the Riviera and
after lunch I played tennis, then began to look for
Mickey and Jeanette. We had all agreed not to eat
between meals because we were going to a big dinner. I looked everywhere and finally found them at a
table in a small sidewalk café in Juan-les Pins. They
were eating huge plates of ice cream and pastry.
Jeanette knew at once that she was caught and she
didn't know where to hide. She was actually blush-
ing.

I began screaming, "For some lousy ice cream
and pastry, you would blow a whole wonderful dinner!"

Jeanette screamed back, "You wouldn't get
this mad if you caught us in bed together!"

"Yes I would," I answered, "*if* you were eating
ice cream and pastry!"

 FRANK SINATRA'S TOMATO SAUCE

SERVES 3 TO 6

*In a frying pan, heat 2 tablespoons olive oil. In it
sauté ¼ onion sliced vertically into thin crescent
wedges and 4 whole peeled cloves of garlic. Sauté until
golden brown and remove garlic.*

*Place the contents of one 1-pound 13-ounce can of
Italian tomatoes in a blender with half of the packing*

*liquid. Mix gently for less than a minute to break up the
pieces. Slowly pour the tomatoes into the frying pan. Be
very careful about spattering hot oil.*

*Stir in ½ teaspoon black pepper, ½ teaspoon salt,
¼ teaspoon oregano and ¼ teaspoon dried basil. Simmer gently, half-covered, for 15 minutes.*

*Pour over 1 pound cooked, hot, well-drained spa-
ghetti and sprinkle with chopped parsley. Grated Ro-
mano or Parmesan cheese can be passed separately.*

CHAPTER SIX

United We Fly

Of humor, E. B. White wrote: "It plays close to the hot fire which is Truth and sometimes the reader feels the heat." Certainly that quality is apparent in the tone and style of Alan King's humor. His role is that of the last angry man, infuriated by the maddening absurdities of everyday situations. The basis of his humor is really nature's inspiring art, there being little need for writers to invent situations when the real world provides them in such abundance. The stories of airline food in this chapter are cases in point, occurring, incredibly and fortunately enough, as we were working on this book. Embellishment was not only unnecessary, but would have been as indecent as obscuring the beauty of an impeccable slice of smoked salmon by showering it with rose petals.

Nor is Alan King's anger feigned, for as he told these stories he became genuinely incensed, pounding the desk, storming about, at times approaching apoplexy.

Having witnessed that nonperformance, I am inclined
to think his stage anger is a toned-down version of his
true feelings. Airlines, take note.

I N THE COURSE OF THIS CHAPTER THE
reader will come across frequent references to
"the road." It should be known that that means any
place between New York and Los Angeles.

Having spent a good part of my life on the road,
I know what Napoleon meant when he said an army
marches on its stomach. So does a comedian. And
considering the kind of food available on the road
these days, it's a miracle I can do a show when I arrive. We've made a lot of progress with cooking in
this country and now you can find good meals in almost any town or city. The problem comes when
you want to eat en route. Getting there is no fun at
all.

There used to be very good food on the road
when I drove. It was not fancy or ambitious but
simple and good. There were all the small diners instead of the franchised chain restaurants with
themes — an elf takes your order after you've been
seated by a clown. Those old diners could handle
anything, whether it was a car with two or three
guys or a bus load with a band. The one short-order
cook would take a look around, listen to orders, and
then working quietly but steadily, without ever
seeming to rush, he got everything out at the same
time. It was always a lanky, wrinkled red-faced kid

who wore a paper hat and looked like Buddy Ebsen.

The tastes I miss from those days are the scrambled eggs done on the same griddle as the bacon, and the home fries with onion that oozed pinkish, paprika-tinted grease. And then there were the big puffy jelly doughnuts that broke open and looked like a wound, bleeding strawberry jam. If you didn't know the diner in those days, and wanted to be sure the eggs weren't powdered, you ordered "country scrambled." For that, the unbeaten eggs were opened directly onto the hot griddle and then scrambled after some white had begun to form. That's a special taste and I make eggs that way sometimes. Because you see the white and the yellow, you know they are fresh.

The short-order cook who makes the world's best scrambled eggs now is not on the highway, but behind the counter of the coffee shop in the Beverly Hills Hotel. Everyone calls him "Red," but his name is Gerhard Bantle and he's been at that job, paper hat and all, since 1959. He makes terrific egg salad, pancakes and the flattest, crispest bacon I ever saw. And if you ask for a toasted bagel, it is hollowed out, then toasted and filled with cream cheese.

But the eggs are the best, much like a soufflé omelet. Red prepares them with a routine so precise and solemn it approaches a religious ritual. He takes two jumbo eggs, cracks them into a small cereal bowl and then ladles melted clarified butter into a seven-inch Wearever aluminum skillet. As the butter heats, he beats the eggs with a fork, over and over again, until they are thin and foamy on top and have lots of air in them. That's the secret. Then he pours them into the hot pan and from that point on, he never lets them alone. He keeps tipping and rotating the pan with his right hand, and with his left (because he is left-handed) he holds the fork and keeps nudging the eggs. He semi-scrambles them and at the same time pulls the cooked edges in from the sides of the pan as though he were making an omelet. Once in a while he folds the egg over so that it sets but never browns. Then he turns it over onto a warm plate. He doesn't add salt or any liquid to the eggs.

The best meals I have while traveling these days are those I eat in the back of my car coming home from an engagement. I always go home if I'm within three hours of New York. I pack before the last show and order a box supper from the hotel kitchen. Usually the chef packs some roast chicken or sliced rare roast beef, good bread, a couple of pickles and maybe a piece of cheese. Then I steal some pillows. I have quite a collection. I prop myself up in the back seat, where I also have some white wine in a plastic cooler. While Dave Flaim, my chauffeur, drives, I eat and then sleep. It all tastes better because I know I'm on my way home. It's a reward I look forward to all during the engagement.

Of all the moveable feasts I ever had, the one I remember best was a catered meal in an ambulance. I wasn't a patient, but I might have been if I had refused to comply with a very special request. I

was playing the Paramount with Billy Eckstein, who
was at the peak of his career. We did eight shows a
day and had about an hour and a half between
them. One day, I got a call from some friend of a
big-time racketeer in New Jersey. He wanted me to
entertain at his daughter's wedding and I was informed that this was not a request. It was a command performance. I explained that I had only an
hour and a half to eat and rest between shows and
he assured me I would be able to do both.

He made me the proverbial offer I couldn't refuse. He said it would help my career. I'd be allowed
to go on living so I could continue it. Naturally I
agreed and left the theater at the appointed hour the
following night. I looked everywhere for a limou-
sine, but all I saw was a double-parked ambulance
and I asked a guy, who looked like the driver, who
was sick. "You will be if you don't get into that ambulance right now," he answered. So I got in and
suddenly the red light started going around on top
of the ambulance and the siren was screaming. But
the guy did it all with style. He had lovely platters of
smoked salmon, sturgeon and a tin of caviar, some
thin slices of pumpernickel and a bottle of Russian
vodka in an ice bucket. I did a twenty-minute show
and when I got back into the ambulance, I found
pastries and espresso. I thanked God that I was not
going back in a hearse. With guys like that, you just
hope they don't serve finger sandwiches; they might
be made with your own fingers.

Of course these days when you talk about eating while traveling, it almost always means airline food. Believe me, that's no joking matter. People think I made up stories about airline food for my act, but I could never create the kind of food they serve. We may have put a man on the moon, but we haven't learned how to come up with decent food on a plane. I usually brown-bag it, with simple, cold food that can be good under such circumstances. I don't know why the airlines can't do that. Good cold food like ham and cheese and fruit. It doesn't have to be hot. Even when they do sandwiches, they're awful because I think they freeze them.

Naturally they describe it all in fancy language and it sounds so good you want to eat the menu. But when the food comes, it's always terrible. Things like those Caesar salads made with artificial garlic and lemon juice and the beef they carve in the cabin that's the same blue color as the cleanser in the toilet bowl.

It can be done right because it works on the Concorde and it has nothing to do with the fare. First class is expensive enough to cover the cost of the food served even on the Concorde, and they do it in very limited space. You know something different is going on from the minute you enter the terminal. They take your coat and before you board the plane there's a nice small buffet with pâtés and cheeses and a full bar. The hors d'oeuvres are beautiful and by the time you board the plane you feel as if you had entered some hospitable home.

Japan Air Lines also proves that good food can

be turned out on a plane. Jeanette and I recently flew that line first-class and they offered two complete menus — one Japanese, the other European for every meal. Jeanette's sushi looked so beautiful and fresh, I almost tried one. I got a grip on myself just in time. But generally the meals served on airlines should be classified as moving violations. When the stewardess tells passengers what to do in case of emergencies, how to use the oxygen and the life vests, the one thing she does not mention is the food. She could suggest that passengers throw the food directly into those little white paper bags *before* eating it. The problem is that they try to do what they can't possibly do well. All that overcooked meat and thick gravy and powdered mashed potatoes and soggy vegetables. And the list of ingredients on the salad dressing packet sounds more like a prescription than a recipe.

What I want to know is, who is the person who approves the food before it is put on the plane? What kind of person could take a taste and say, "O.K. Load it"? I know this: he's someone who is not going to take that plane but who will get in a car and drive home to a good meal. He's either a maniac or a misanthrope. Probably both.

One of my big regrets in life is that I never took a trip on great ships such as the *Ile de France* where the food was said to have been wonderful. But last year I took a four-day cruise on the *QE2* from Aruba to Florida. I got on midway through the trip and was pleasantly surprised to find Barbara Walters there.

She had been aboard a week and knew all the ropes. She explained dinner in the grill, saying that if I didn't like anything on the menu I could order anything I wanted. It was all magnificent.

But getting down to Aruba was something else. I was on American Airlines Flight 679, leaving at ten in the morning. The menu said "Breakfast," meaning, I assumed, the first meal of the day. The first course was melon with prosciutto and brie, on an empty stomach. Then came a seafood omelet covered with a cheese cream sauce. Potatoes au gratin (with cream and cheese) were there, along with sautéed eggplant, tomatoes and onions, again with grated cheese. The only thing that didn't have cheese was the coffee, but it was served with a cheese Danish. You don't know what constipation is until you've had a seven-course cheese breakfast. The only thing that saved me was the tap water in Aruba.

But the best was yet to come. After landing at Fort Lauderdale, I flew home on Delta's Flight 1052 on January 2, 1984. It was one hour late leaving and I was so starved I was even looking forward to airline food. It was crowded — five passengers oversold and I was the last first-class passenger to arrive. And because I smoke, I sat in the last seat of the front cabin. All of the first-class food orders were mixed up and everyone got the wrong meal. Except me. When she got to me, the stewardess announced that there was no food left. They were short by exactly one first-class meal.

The whole cabin crew was buzzing and bowing around me, pouring drinks and apologizing. About twenty minutes later, the stewardess reappears, beaming triumphantly. "Mr. King," she says, "I found something for you to eat." With that she holds out a small plastic tray with a thin, greasy sandwich on a piece of crumbled foil.

"What is that?" I ask, or probably screamed.

"It's a peanut butter and banana sandwich," she says.

I figured this must be April Fool's Day and that friends were pulling a gag on me. And gag was just the word. I said, "No, thank you. I won't eat it. But I will take it with me so I can have it bronzed. Otherwise, no one will believe me." As I left the plane, the captain tried to make amends and he offered me a smuggled-in Cuban cigar. I ate it.

The next day I called Delta and pretended to book a flight to Fort Lauderdale and I said I wanted to order a special meal. What kind did they have? The reservation clerk reeled off nine kinds of special meals for first-class passengers — vegetarian, kosher, dairy, no salt, low cholesterol, a fruit plate, a sandwich, and so on. I asked if I could have a peanut butter and banana sandwich. She said there was no such meal available. I kept insisting and finally she switched me to a supervisor. "I don't mean to be difficult," I said, "but I'd like a peanut butter and banana sandwich. I had it on a previous flight." She said she would check and call me back. Two days later she reported back, saying that they had checked the flight log and found that the sandwich was brought on board by a kid's mother and that he refused to eat it. So they put it on a tray for me.

Now who could make up a story like that?

🌿 PEANUT BUTTER AND BANANA SANDWICH "READY WHEN YOU ARE"

For each serving you will need two slices of standard, soft all-American white bread. Chill peanut butter until it is too stiff to spread. Place about 2 tablespoons on one slice of the bread and attempt to spread, making sure you tear the slice of bread in at least three places. Slice a very overripe banana and place on top of the peanut butter. Top with the second slice of bread and cut in half diagonally. You will want the thin corners so they can crumble off. Wrap the sandwich in waxed paper, then in foil and place it in your mother's handbag, wedging it in between her compact and her cigarettes. She must carry it around for at least three hours. This sandwich improves with age much the way certain wines and brandies improve on an ocean voyage back and forth across the equator. Then partially unwrap, place on a plastic tray and serve to Alan King when he is starving. And stand back!

CHAPTER SEVEN

 Room Service,

Por Favor . . .

Many hotels are reluctant to have actors as guests and this chapter explains why. Throughout Alan King's telling of it, I was surprised that he would own up to some of the pranks. Yet he told each with what I suspect is the sort of verve and sense of mad adventure that accounted for their happening in the first place.

To anyone who travels a lot, room service can be the ultimate luxury or the ultimate frustration. What could be more comforting and elegant than to be dressed in a robe, sitting in a plush chair and being served some marvelous meal in complete privacy? What could be worse than being trapped in a room at the mercy of an inefficient, bureaucratic room service staff dishing up lukewarm convenience foods?

That both are possible is obvious from this chapter, as is King's complete candor. He is willing to risk looking like the villain, in the interest of keeping the record straight.

THERE ARE TWO THINGS MOST HOTELS
do not do well: room service and laundry. Of the
two, the last is usually hopeless, so much so that I always take my dirty shirts home to be laundered.
Otherwise they come back wrapped in cellophane
with a picture of two bluebirds chirping, "Good
Morning. We have screwed up your laundry again."
With room service you have a fighting chance, but
only if you do as I do. As soon as I get to a hotel, I
find the day and night room-service captains and I
give them each $10. After that they'd kill for me.
They might even be sure my coffee arrives hot.
Then when I call, I ask for one of them by name.
Otherwise you call room service and hear "One moment, please . . ." And then the recorded music
starts. Who needs it? It's either too early to dance, or
I'm too tired. The next thing you hear is "There will
be a two-hour wait for room service. Have a nice
day."

I never like to hang those tags on the outside
doorknob for my breakfast order, either. Suppose I
have an exotic dream and want a breakfast to fit my
mood? Even more, I'm always afraid of what will
happen, mostly because I judge others by myself.
Whenever I go back to my room late at night and see
shoes in the hall to be polished, I love to mix them
up. I guess I'm just a louse. I even look at everyone's
breakfast tag and if I don't like what was ordered, I
change it.

Once I did fill in the tag and hung it outside.
But Jeanette went to bed after I did and she hung a

Do Not Disturb sign over the order. I woke up at eight and was eagerly awaiting my breakfast. Two hours later I thought I'd check and looked outside. There was a note from the hotel: "We find it impossible to serve you breakfast without disturbing you."

Many hotels now offer room service twenty-four hours a day, which means they can aggravate you around the clock. Before that you could starve after ten or eleven. Many's the time I've needed a hamburger at three in the morning and the only way to get it was to send a cab driver for it. Between the round-trip fare, the tip to the bellboy and the price of the burger, a midnight snack could cost about $40, but when you're hungry, you're hungry.

Scrambled eggs are probably the biggest test of room service. I gave up ordering them long ago because either they're overdone and look like grayish-yellow sponges, or they're loose on top and dry on the bottom, like bits of blotter soaked in liquid. Once, though, I learned how good they could be. It was at the Ritz in Madrid, one of the world's great hotels. In fact, it was so great that they didn't allow actors in. That was because John Wayne and some friends had once gotten drunk and attacked the hotel. When they left, it looked like the Alamo after the fall. But through good connections and a phony passport, I got a room. After I was there for a few days, I was in the cocktail lounge and the manager came by. He very politely said that it was brought to his attention that I was not taking advantage of breakfast in my room.

"We are very proud of our room service, Mr. King, and I wondered why," he said.

I answered, "Well, to be honest, I like scrambled eggs and usually they're awful when they're sent up from a kitchen."

"Mr. King," he said, pleading with me, "order scrambled eggs in your room tomorrow." He was so sincere, I felt obliged to do so.

About ten minutes after I called in my order, up comes a captain in formal dining-room dress and with him a waiter pushing a gueridon. On it were all sorts of copper pans, whisks, bowls and three little glass dishes holding minced parsley, chives and grated cheese. The waiter breaks three eggs into the bowl, using only one hand to do that and then puts a big lump of whipped butter in the skillet. The captain meanwhile is whisking the eggs, asking me if I want chives or parsley or cheese in them. Then he pours in a touch of heavy cream from a silver pitcher and seasons the eggs by grinding not only fresh pepper, but sea salt as well. He pours the eggs into the pan with the frothing butter and begins to gentle the eggs and tip the pan, turning them out onto a warmed plate exactly as I wanted them. It was like watching a ballet. That afternoon I went to the manager's office to thank him for the "special attention." "It was not special at all, Mr. King," he said. "That is our standard procedure." Now that's room service.

Another one of my favorite hotels is La Reserve in Beaulieu in the south of France. The first time I saw it I wanted to get in, but I had heard that was impossible. Six of us were staying nearby at the Hôtel de Paris in Monte Carlo and my old pal John Mills invited us all to lunch at La Reserve, where he was vacationing. The table was set on the terrace overlooking the pool and the sea. Women looked beautiful in those silky colorful Pucci dresses and it was like a scene in an old Cary Grant movie. In addition to Jeanette and me, guests at our table were Tony Martin and his wife, Cyd Charisse; Mr. and Mrs. David Niven, who had come over from their home in Saint-Jean-Cap-Ferrat; Billy Rose, who was between wives; and good friends of his, Mr. and Mrs. Fred Weinstock. Fred was a New York merchant prince (in the rag business) who for fifteen years spent every summer at La Reserve; he just made reservations from one year to the next.

David Niven looked immaculate in his open shirt with ascot. As soon as we were introduced, I asked him something I had always wanted to know. "How do you tie an ascot so it stays in place?" I had tried many times, but with my short 16½" neck and not much of the ascot, it kept sliding around and coming undone. "My dear boy," he answered, "there's nothing to it. Look!" With that he flips up the front of the ascot and there was a strip of Scotch tape holding the underside to his chest. Now that's class!

"I'm in love with this whole hotel. How can I get in?" I asked Jeanette.

"Buy it," she answered.

Even the food was perfect, beginning with the beautiful salade Niçoise made of raw, pale green vegetables — sliced tiny artichoke hearts, those small green fava beans, olives, fresh tuna. Unbelievable. Then we had the fish, loup de mer, grilled over branches of flaming fennel. Finally, as the afternoon wore on, M. Potfer, the owner, came by and John Mills asked him to have a glass of wine with us. After telling him how much I admired his hotel, I suddenly found myself switching to what Jeanette calls my continental pluperfect subjunctive conditional — my idea of talking classy. It's the reason that even people who speak English do not understand me in Europe.

"If one were thinking of possibly staying here, what might one have to do?"

A glint came into his eye as he answered, "Mr. King. Someone has to die."

That evening we were all back at the Hôtel de Paris and the men were in the cocktail lounge waiting for the women. Billy Rose was called to the phone and he returned, looking sad.

"Fred Weinstock's mother died today in New York. He's going back for the funeral," Rose announced.

Sympathetic though I was, I went straight to the phone and called M. Potfer. "Remember me? Alan King? I was with John Mills this afternoon?" I said.

"Of course, Mr. King. What might one be able to do for you?" At last, I thought, a man who speaks my language.

"Well, remember what you said about someone

dying? Mr. Weinstock's mother died in New York
and he'll be going back for two weeks," I said.

"Mr. King, be here at ten in the morning," he
said.

Naturally I get there at eight-fifteen the next
morning and as soon as the bags are in the room I
begin looking around. What I wanted was something like a coffee shop — a place to have an early
breakfast when Jeanette sleeps late. M. Potfer saw
me and sensed I was looking for something.

"Can one help you, Mr. King?" he asked.

"If one were thinking that one might want an
early breakfast not in one's room, where could one
expect to find it?" I asked.

"Anywhere one would like," he said, indicating
the lobby, the lounge, the garden patio or the pool-
side terrace. Now that's a hotel!

Some time later we really put him to the test.
We had been at a big party at the Château Madrid
up on the top of the Grande Corniche. Coming
down, our car broke down and we couldn't get help.
So we walked down the mountain and it took several
hours. We got back to La Reserve at five in the
morning, all scratched up and starved. I asked the
concierge if it was possible to get something to eat.

"I'll see what I can dig up," he said. "Why
don't you go to your room and get comfortable?"

Next thing we know, in came big silver trays
with pâtés, poached eggs in aspic, cold rare roast
beef, salads and fresh, warm rolls that had just been
baked for breakfast. With that was a chilled bottle of

Puligny-Montrachet and thin flutes. Now that's digging!

None of my room-service experiences have been more elegant, but some have been more colorful. Many years ago, Tony Martin and I were doing a show for the Harvest Moon Ball, an annual benefit in Chicago hosted by Irv Kupcinet, the columnist for the *Sun-Times*. With us was Hal Bourne, who was then Tony Martin's conductor and accompanist. We got there as a blizzard began and went to our suite in the Ambassador East Hotel. The storm got so bad, the benefit was postponed for a day and we were trapped. The suite had a living room and, on each side of that, a bedroom. Martin and I shared one bedroom and Hal had the other. The living room was full of liquor, fruit, cheese and candy, but by midafternoon we were stir-crazy — also drunk. We could see a big chimney stack across the court from our window and I bet Martin $5 that he couldn't hit the stack with a piece of fruit. Hal, who was a civilized adult, sensed what was coming and said, "Don't be children." But the contest began and we were throwing apples, pears, oranges, everything at the chimney.

At one point, Martin yells that he hit the chimney and that I owe him $5.

"C'mon," I said. "You're just getting old and your eyes are bad."

"Old?" he yells. "I'll show you old!" And with that he threw a glass of water at me. Not to be outdone, I picked up a pitcher of water and threw it at him. Bourne now decides to get the hell out of there and locks himself in his bedroom. Martin starts to chase me around the room with more water and I duck into my bedroom and lock the door. A few minutes later, Martin knocks on my door.

"Fingers," he calls pleadingly. "All is forgiven. I'm lonesome in here."

Not trusting him, I climb up on a chair and look over the transom. Sure enough, he's standing there with a pitcher full of water, ready to let go. "Just a second," I call back as I go for a glass of water. I got back on the chair and poured it down through the transom, all over him.

Meanwhile, Bourne is oblivious to the fact that the War of the Waters has escalated. He decides to order food from room service. Soon the waiter arrives, dressed like a blackamoor with a turban and satin pantaloons — the hotel's costume. Bourne, of course, gave the suite number for the order and so the waiter knocks on the living-room door.

Martin asks, "Who is it?"

A booming, resonant black voice answers, "Room service, suh."

Now Martin is sure it's me and says in a sweet little Red Riding Hood voice, "Just a moment, please." He fills a pitcher, opens the door and throws the water in the waiter's face. It took a lot of hundred dollar bills to dry that guy off.

I also once shared a suite with my partner, Walter Hyman (he of the Orange Julius). We traveled to Los Angeles to produce a Barbra Streisand tour. Hyman was one of the sweetest guys in the world even though he had many idiosyncrasies. One was that he despised creamed chipped beef. Couldn't stand the consistency, the look or the smell. It reminded him of being back in the army, where it was known affectionately as S.O.S. — shit on a shingle. If he was in a restaurant and saw it being served anywhere in the room, he'd get up and leave, making a quick pit stop at the men's room. He was also a guy who couldn't go to sleep before three in the morning and therefore who could not get up until noon. In between, he was the world's lightest sleeper.

He also had to have a refrigerator filled with Orange Crush soda that he could drink during the night and he kept the room as cold and dark as Siberia. He hung double blackout curtains and had their edges taped to the wall. Naturally I didn't want to share his gulag and we had separate bedrooms. Even so, when I got up at seven, no matter how quiet I tried to be, he heard me. Do you know what it's like not to be able to flush a toilet until noon? After two days, he announced he was changing his room. The only thing he could get was a bungalow at $1,000 a day but he felt it was well worth it.

The first morning he's in it, I get a call from one of our associates in New York, where it's three hours later. He needs an immediate decision on something and it's only seven-thirty in L.A. I decided to call Hyman. He screams at the top of his lungs, "Don't you know it's seven-thirty in the morning?" But I get his O.K. before he slams the phone down.

Next morning negotiations were accelerating and I get another call — only later — 7:45 A.M. Again I try to call Hyman, but this time the operator won't put me through. "Mr. King," she says, "Mr. Hyman left strict orders. Under no condition is he to be disturbed." I plead with her and tell her it's an emergency and she puts me through. Now Walter goes berserk.

"If you can't wait until noon for your decisions, maybe I should get another partner," he yells.

"Make sure he's a night burglar so he keeps the same hours you do," I answer. During the day he warns the manager to instruct all operators not to put calls through to him before noon even if the hotel is on fire and especially if it's Alan King calling.

The third morning the same thing happens and it's even more urgent, but nothing I tried would work. I was desperate and figured we would lose the deal. But suddenly I got an idea. I called room service and said, "This is Walter Hyman in bungalow Seven H. I'm having a breakfast meeting. Could you quickly send me eight orders of creamed chipped beef along with Orange Crush and coffee? And if I don't answer the doorbell right away I may be in the shower, so tell the waiter to bang hard on the door."

So on that cold, damp morning I ran out to the grounds in front of his bungalow and hid in the bushes. But I had a clear view of the path, the porch and the front door of the bungalow. Pretty soon here comes this wagon train — two waiters and two bus-boys lifting tables and gueridons with silver, dishes, a coffee urn, Orange Crush and a big copper caul-dron of chipped beef up onto the porch. The waiter rings the bell and when there is no answer, he fol-lows instructions and pounds like a madman.

From inside comes a piercing scream: "WHO IS IT?"

"Your breakfast, sir," comes the answer.

"My WHAT?" he screams back and with that he pulls the door open with such force he almost tears off the hinges. "What the hell is going on out here?" he shouts, and with that lifts the cover off the cauldron and looks down.

"It's your chipped beef for eight," the waiter answers helpfully.

With that, Hyman goes crazy and in one sweep of his arms knocks the cauldron of chipped beef off the wagon. "King?" he bellows. "I know you're out there. If I ever find you, I'll kill you." And there were the waiters gazing down at their splattered trousers, ankle-deep in creamed chipped beef. Now that's shit on a shingle!

The real problem with most room service is that the customer is a captive, so the management doesn't think it's necessary to try hard. That's espe-cially true in a hospital, which is why, I think, food there is so terrible. After I had been in *The Impossi-ble Years* for a little over a year, I once spent ten days in a hospital for what they called "complete exhaus-tion." Complete exhaustion is a rich man's disease.

I've never heard of a poor man being admitted to a hospital for that ailment. I was in for a lot of tests, and, because I could afford it, I had nurses around the clock. I knew I had arrived.

The two day nurses did absolutely nothing, but the night nurse had a hectic schedule. She did needlepoint and during the ten days I was there, she made an entire couch right before my eyes. Her most annoying trait was that she treated me like a child or an idiot. When she came on each evening, she greeted me with "How are we feeling? Did we enjoy our din-din?"

"I don't know about you," I used to answer, "but my food stank." When she left at dawn, she would put down my brecky-wecky tray.

Having had gallons of blood taken out of me and tubes sticking out of every hole in my body, I'd had it with the hospital and with this Florence Nightingale. I warned that if she didn't stop the baby talk, her services would no longer be required. She went to the head of medicine, who happened to be my brother, and complained that Alan King was the worst patient she ever attended.

He rushed in and with the typical Kniberg voice started screaming, "Why the hell are you offending the nurses and disrupting the entire hospital?"

Ten decibels higher, I informed him that I was not a piece of meat or an idiot and I did not eat din-din or brecky-wecky.

"Save your goddam jokes for TV," my brother said. "Just lie there and behave yourself."

Every morning on my brecky-wecky tray there was a glass of apple juice. Now it is very important that you understand this. I don't dislike apple juice. I hate it. I can't stand the taste, the texture, the color or the smell. Every night, having nothing else to do, I would fill out the menus for the next day, where you're supposed to circle, check, cross or underline your choices. Never once did I circle, check, cross or underline apple juice. But every morning, there it was. Being my father's son, I decided revenge was in order.

One of the worst things about being in the hospital is that morning urine analysis that requires a sample. Just before dawn, you hear the tinkling of the urine vials coming down the hall. Everyone has to fill a bottle, even the mailman. One morning after my nurse had given me my brecky-wecky tray and left, I took the apple juice and poured it into the urine vial. I immediately felt relieved. (One giant step for mankind!)

My only regret was that I would not be in the lab when they analyzed the specimen. Five minutes later, in walks my nurse. She picks up the vial, shakes it violently and in the age-old method of testing, she holds it up to the light of the window. "My, my," she says. "We're a little cloudy this morning, aren't we?"

"Oh, yes?" I said. "Maybe we should run it through again." I drank it and she fainted. It was one room service brecky-wecky I'll never forget.

In the fifties and sixties, my idea of a perfect vacation was a stay at Villa Vera, a marvelous hotel

in Acapulco. It had not yet been spoiled by tourism
and you could see the whole bay from the hotel bal-
conies. Now all you see is twenty other hotels. But I
loved all of Mexico and went whenever I got the
chance. My only frustration was that I could not understand the language and in those days very few
Mexicans spoke English. It bothered me especially
when ordering food and I would complain about the
waiters not learning English. "Why don't you learn
Spanish?" Jeanette asked, logically. The only words
I could say were "buenos días, buenos tardes,
buenas noches, muchas gracias, mantequilla,"
which means butter, "cenicero," which is ashtray,
and "cáscara de limón" — a twist of lemon peel.
Now that doesn't make much of a meal. I decided to
take the toro by the horns and learn Spanish so that
the next time we went I could stun everyone. For a
year I took lessons secretly at Berlitz and in between
went to restaurants in New York like Toledo, the
Spanish Pavilion and Mexican Gardens, just so I
could practice with the waiters and busboys. Finally
we planned a trip — Jeanette and me and our
friends Phyllis and Bill Dorman. As soon as we land
at the airport in Acapulco, I shout, "Prendez usted
el equipaje, por favor." Sure enough, two porters
picked up our luggage. I was not the only one who
was surprised. "Just a little something I picked up
in the Barrio," I said.

When we get to the Villa Vera, I decide to call
room service to stock the terrace bar. I pick up the
phone and the operator says, "Hola!"

I ask, in Spanish, "Room service?"

"Si," comes the answer.

Then I proceed to order tequila, gin, vodka, soda, ice, all in Spanish. Now Jeanette and the Dormans are wide-eyed and I'm beginning to feel like Ricardo Montalban. Already all the money spent at Berlitz seems worthwhile. Soon the stuff arrives exactly as ordered, but with one addition — four bottles of beer stuck in a bucket of ice.

"Beer?" Bill Dorman says. "Who needs beer?"

I don't know either, of course, but don't want to admit it. "Listen. Don't you know the Mexicans are so proud of their Carta Blanca beer that they send some along to get you to try it?" I say.

Next morning we wake up and everyone asks me to order breakfast. I pick up the phone and again hear "Hola!" and again I ask, "Room service?" and again get a "Si." Then I order — four orders of assorted tropical melon, four huevos rancheros, four coffees. Sure enough, it all arrives — four melons, four huevos rancheros, four coffees and . . . four bottles of beer.

"Who the hell drinks beer for breakfast?" Bill Dorman asks.

"They know me from past visits," I say, "and they figure I'll need it for my hangover." Well, for the next three days, every time I order room service I get the four bottles of beer. Soon there were forty bottles in our rooms, scattered everywhere, and I was thinking up ways to use them. I took beer shampoos, recommended beer foot baths for tired feet and dabbed it all over myself as a cure for mosquito bites. I almost had everyone convinced it was the best lotion for a bad sunburn.

On the fourth day I was having a drink at the patio bar talking to my old friend, the bartender, Miguel. After my fourth margarita, I decided to confide in him.

"Amigo mío," I began. "Amigo mío, as you can see I have learned to speak the Spanish fluently. Nevertheless, someone in room service is screwing me. Every time I order room service, I get what I wanted plus something I did not order." He tells me to go through my routine exactly as I did, "I pick up the phone," I say, "and the operator answers 'Hola!' Then I ask for room service in Spanish, 'Cuatro services,' and I give my order."

Then Miguel interrupts, "And you get four bottles of beer!"

"How the hell did you know that?" I ask.

He says, "Because that's what it sounds like you're ordering. 'Cuatro' is four. Room is 'cuarto.' And your 'services' sounds to them like the word for beer — 'cervezas.' "

I walk away, mumbling, "What the hell does a Mexican know about Spanish, anyway?" I thought it must have been my Castilian lisp.

POSTSCRIPT

The explanation of the beer–room service mix-up represents a few of the most difficult sentences we've had to work out for this book. I suspected that Alan King still has a hard time differentiating be-

tween cuatro and cuarto. Sure enough, when I mentioned it to Jeanette, she said, "We still always get four beers every time he orders room service in Spain or Mexico."

 ## CREAMED CHIPPED BEEF

SERVES 4 TO 6

As it happens, both Alan King and I actually like creamed chipped beef despite its lowbrow reputation. Together we worked out the following recipe, which we think lifts it considerably above its S.O.S. designation.

Shred about 8 ounces (half a pound) of dried beef and soak it for 5 or 10 minutes in hot water. Drain the meat thoroughly on a paper towel.

Heat 5 tablespoons unsalted butter in a skillet and in it sauté 4 tablespoons of finely minced onion until soft but not brown. Add the beef and sauté for about 5 minutes. Add 2 tablespoons of brandy, warm for a minute and then ignite. When flames die down, sprinkle in 2 tablespoons of flour and stir until flour disappears. Let cook slowly for 5 minutes.

Pour in 2½ cups hot, scalded half-and-half (milk and cream) and bring to a boil. Reduce heat and simmer 10 minutes, adding more half-and-half as needed and seasoning to taste with Worcestershire sauce, black pepper and salt. Add a handful of minced parsley and, finally, stir in 3 hard-boiled eggs that have been peeled and quartered vertically.

Spoon over 4 to 6 toasted, buttered English muffin halves and sprinkle each portion with parsley.

CHAPTER EIGHT

Guess Who's Not Coming to Dinner

When we discussed a title for this chapter on being a host, Alan King thought it should be called "Caring." He might also express it as "Fresh rolls," for the buying of rolls by the host himself, just before the meal, seems to be his mark of real caring. If hospitality were not so benign a pursuit, Alan might be described as obsessive about his attention to detail and his desire to anticipate and solve any problem that could arise. Much of that intensity stems from generosity and, of course, from pride in what he has achieved and how much he has learned.

Alan plans parties with equal earnestness whether they are simple or grand, at home or away. As an entertainer who has made a great deal of money, he does at times entertain lavishly, but he also does wonderful, simple, festive dinners with inexpensive flowers and food. He takes as much pride in serving his turkey with crazy eggs or barbecued spareribs as a classic rack of

*lamb persillé. To that extent, his own concerns on party
planning offer much useful advice for almost anyone.
    Some people throw parties, others give them. Alan
King produces them with the same professional attention to detail he exerts when producing plays or films.
He is serious about it. ("Being serious is a step up," he
says.) He will interrupt a business meeting to check on
the bakery or to call his wife to be sure the staff and the
florist know their roles.*

*It seems almost like a game, or a challenge, to see
just how much delight he can work into the visual and
culinary effects of the evening. Being a guest at his
home is a very special experience. Nothing is left to
chance. With the invitation comes a map, precisely
drawn, so that there will not be a long search for his
home on Long Island. If the party is large, he has
moonlighting midshipmen from the nearby U.S. Merchant Marine Academy as parking attendants.*

*The setting for parties is his great rambling
Tudor-style house on the edge of Long Island Sound.
Built for Oscar Hammerstein II, the house has been dec-
orated by Melanie Kahane in a bright, stylish and very
personal way. The Kings also built what they alternately call a guest or summer house. Linked to the main
house by a cobblestone mews, the summer house's focal
point is a huge living room, with a bar, comfortable
chaises and lounge chairs and glass walls overlooking
the Sound. The room is a veritable photograph album,
full of pictures of family, friends and celebrities the
Kings have met and entertained. In addition to a huge
fireplace, the living room also conceals a film projector
and screen, and showing movies is one of Alan's favorite after-dinner entertainments. For big parties, the*

*room is cleared of furniture and many tables are set up,
along with a bandstand and a dance floor.*

*That house is always used at some point during a
party. The evening may start there with cocktails and
end with coffee and drinks, while the main course is
served in the main house, or the order can be reversed.
"We're moving to a clean house for dinner" is the way
Alan likes to put it.*

*Because Alan thinks of a party as a theatrical pro-
duction, he expects something from his audience. If he
could, he would even write his guests' parts. He is disappointed at heavy, pre-dinner drinkers who dull their
palates. He is edgy if anyone at the table is so deep in
conversation that the food is allowed to grow cold on the
plate. He becomes furious at dieters who will not try at
least a little of everything. But he is considerate of those
who cannot eat something because of health problems.*

*His view of inattentive guests is much like that of
an actor who hears coughs and whispers in the audience. I have even seen a look of annoyance flicker across
Alan's face when a guest dropped a glass that smashed
on the dance floor. He brushed off the incident with a
wave of his hand, but there had been that quick tight-
ening of his upper lip and the clenching of his teeth
when it happened. It was not in the plan, it was a flaw
in the evening and it was beyond his control.*

THE GREATEST DISPLAYS OF HOSPI-
tality are always in the homes of self-made
men — those who started with very little and
achieved great things. Perhaps that's because they
grew up during the Depression when the smallest

thing meant a lot and no one had much to give. Or because they were first-generation Americans imbued with their parents' European idea of hospitality. I remember, in my mother's house, no one could come in without being offered a cup of tea or coffee and a piece of freshly baked cake — something for their comfort. And no matter how much money these people have made, or how large their staffs may be, they look into things themselves. It's like the host pouring wine into a guest's empty glass even though there are waiters to do it. Or knocking on guest-room doors to see if people have everything they need. Sure, there are eighty maids to do it, but it's the host who really cares.

For example, parties given by Barbara and Frank Sinatra are like Italian weddings and it is a special privilege to be invited to their Palm Springs home for Christmas Eve. Guests are a mix of old friends, family and a lot of priests. Frank is completely democratic (even since he became a Republican) about inviting guests, and along with friends, such as Walter Annenberg, there is likely to be Frank's favorite parking attendant from his country club who happens to be alone that night. All are obviously equally welcome.

The food is incredible and more than enough for the hundred or so people. There are always four pastas of different kinds, an endless antipasto, whole legs of roast veal and gigantic turkeys stuffed with Italian sausages and chestnuts. After the meal there is a private midnight mass. Frank doesn't fool around. Trying to cover his bets, he even insists that before the meal, I recite the Hebrew blessings for bread and wine.

Another dedicated host is Irwin Winkler, the producer of the "Rocky" movies and *The Right Stuff*, among other films. He and his wife, Margo, live in Beverly Hills and are true gourmets. They're the only people I know who go to Paris, rent an apartment, hire a great chef, then eat out. Their parties are always food adventures. Their twenty-fifth anniversary was one of Irwin's greatest productions. Bobby Short flew out to entertain and Chasen's did fantastic catering. Adding to the spectacle of the evening was the buffet-table centerpiece sent by film magnate Jerry Perenchio: twenty-five magnums of Dom Pérignon banked with flowers, in an enormous silver bowl.

One of the high points in my year is the summer party given by Mary and Peter Stone in East Hampton. Mary is such a great cook she even bakes her own bread. Peter, a playwright who has won an Emmy, an Oscar and a Tony, becomes a sanitarian that day and cleans things before they are dirty. I once fixed up a big plateful of Mary's gorgeous food, then set it down for a second to get a glass of wine. I got back just as Peter was clearing it away. He was in a hurry to get the plate washed before his shaggy dog did it for him.

When I'm in London, I try not to miss the Sunday brunch given by Elliott Kastner, the film producer, and his wife, Tessa, at their home in

Runnymede. It's an all-day soiree with the most interesting guests. Imagine sitting between Roger Moore and Sean Connery — the two James Bonds staring at each other. I felt like 003½. Where else can you look at and listen to Marlon Brando, telling you what's wrong with the world and being right?

The menu begins with bagels, lox, smoked fish, cream cheese and then progresses to haute cuisine. Elliott is a compulsive furniture polisher and keeps going around the room buffing imaginary spots from the furniture. Just to keep him happy, I go around dropping clumps of ashes.

All of these hosts know there are many ways of showing guests you care that have nothing to do with money. Jeanette and I always get up and walk around during a meal, asking if guests want anything. And if we have dinner at one long table, she and I switch seats so each of us can talk to all of our guests. We are also careful about the waiters we hire because so many of our guests are writers, actors and producers. Most part-time waiters are actors nowadays and if they hear that there are producers at the party they become impossible — singing "Reach Out and Touch Someone" in Diana Ross's ear or pretending to be a hunchback and reciting lines from *Richard III* while serving Joe Papp.

One thing we never do is give a theme party, unless it just happens. That's when I invite a doctor or a lawyer or a psychiatrist and guests line up to have their problems solved. It's called a free advice party. Some theme! There are better ways to be entertaining, mainly by being original with food. If I want to serve sausages for appetizers, I group them in a big basket as they do at Au Beaujolais in Paris, where I love to have lunch. I put out all the sausages and some cutting boards with knives and let guests help themselves. You can do that with whole raw vegetables, too. Everyone loves that. And if I'm serving little boiled potatoes scooped out and filled with caviar or minced smoked salmon, I like to offer aquavit instead of the standard drinks. To make it look inviting, I freeze the schnapps bottle in a block of ice, as they do in Scandinavia, and pour it that way.

Sometimes it's effective to combine the lavish with the simple, like serving peasant food at a black-tie party. That's what I did in 1972 for Teddy Kennedy's fortieth birthday. There were a hundred guests and almost as many security agents. Not only did Teddy have the Secret Service but Hugh Carey, then governor, had the state police. Other guests were Adolph Green and his wife, Phyllis Newman, Lena Horne, Betty Comden, the Sidney Lumets and the Frank Giffords, Andy Williams with the most beautiful girl I ever saw, Elizabeth and George Stevens, Jr., Mr. and Mrs. Arthur Schlesinger, Jr., Lauren Bacall, Pat Kennedy Lawford, Jean Kennedy Smith and her husband, Steve, and Ethel Kennedy, who was with Hugh Carey — *"All Democrats!"* The only people Teddy did not know were Sue and Herman Merinoff — *"Republicans!"*

The meal was prepared by my two great cooks, Chica and Manuel, who are Portuguese. We decided that for so many people we would do something informal and we worked out an Iberian meal.

There is a big Portuguese community in Mineola and that's where they did most of the shopping. They bought bacalhua, the dried codfish, and soaked it for days to get the salt out and then made hot, crisp fried croquettes. Those were passed with drinks along with some of the more usual appetizers. Paella was the main course, done in those great big open pans, and the cooks used linguica, the Portuguese sausage, for it and spiced it up with piri, the fiery little chili peppers marinated in olive oil. Instead of the usual birthday cake, we had individual custard tarts that the Portuguese are famous for and nogados — big towers of tiny balls of fried dough covered with honey. It looked wild with a candle stuck on top.

After dinner, Teddy made a very gracious thank-you speech and he tried to be especially nice to the only two strangers — Sue and Herman Merinoff. So he said, "And I especially want to thank my old friends, Herbert and Ceil Lebendorf." They remained Republicans.

Not all of my parties have gone smoothly, of course, and food is not the only thing that can go wrong. The worst crisis came when my son Andy was about nine years old and I was planning a big Sunday brunch and swimming party for forty people around the pool. Andy could never get the water hot enough and whenever he had the chance, he pushed the thermostat up as far as it could go.

I did all of the shopping for the party early on

Saturday morning. I wanted to get it out of the way because it was my father's birthday and I intended to drive up to the Catskills, where he and my mother were staying, to have dinner with them. I knew I'd be home late and didn't want to have too much to do the next morning. I bought grapefruit and oranges to be cut up and added to a pitcher of sangria, and I drove to Tabachnick for just the right cream cheese, Swiss cheese, whitefish, sturgeon, some salmon caviar and Nova Scotia salmon. I prefer belly lox for breakfast, but I thought my guests would like the milder, more sophisticated Novy. I also found perfect, sweet Bermuda onions and the salty black Greek olives, and I checked the garden to be sure we had enough ripe tomatoes. The only thing I left for the next morning were the bialys, bagels and pumpernickel. Remember fresh! That done, I drove up to the country, had dinner with my parents and got home at three o'clock Sunday morning, dead tired but happy that I could rest in the morning.

I don't know what possessed me to go to the pool at that hour, but I did. I couldn't find it. All I saw was a huge mushroom cloud of steam. I finally found the water and it was boiling. I went into the house and started screaming.

Jeanette shushed me. "You'll wake Andy up."

"Wake him up? I'm going to kill him!" I yelled. "What in the hell did you do to the pool?" I asked him. "It's like chicken soup!"

"Then put matzo balls in it," he answered, turning over.

"It's ninety-eight degrees," I said.

"Perfect!" he answered. "Perfect for making tea," I said, "but not for swimming!"

I turned all the heat off and started fresh water running into the pool. I figured by one o'clock, when the guests arrived, it would be cool. I fell into bed and slept but kept dreaming about guests going into the pool and coming out scalded. I woke up at eight and stumbled out to the pool. In five hours it had cooled two degrees. I knew I had to do something, so I looked in the Yellow Pages to find someone selling ice. Finally I called a likely source. An Italian guy answered, "Whadda ya wanna?"

"You sell ice?" I asked.

When he said yes, I told him I'd be right over. When I got there, I realized I was still wearing my pajamas. Sure enough, there were the old-fashioned mountainous blocks of ice and I asked how much they were.

"Ten dollars each," he said, looking at the wild man in front of him.

"Sold!" I answered. "Deliver twenty."

"Whadda ya wanna them for?" he asked.

"What is this, a quiz?" I yelled. "Just put them on a truck and deliver them to my house."

I picked up the bread and rolls and went home to wait.

A few minutes later he arrived with the twenty cakes at $10 each. He must have thought I was having a party for eight hundred people and that Dorothy Hamill was the guest of honor.

"Where da ya wanna the ice?" he asked.

"In the pool," I said. "Throw it in the pool!"

With that he stood back, just staring at me, his forefinger laid along the side of his nose, deep in calculation. "Hey," he said, his eyes brightening. "Hey — wada minuta . . . I knowa you . . . You're from the televish. Allena Funta! Allena Funta! Where's the camera? Where's the camera?" he screamed as he looked up at the pool and in the trees.

"I'm Alana Kinga, not Allena Funta," I pleaded. "Stick the goddam ice in the pool already. It cost me two hundred dollars and it's melting in the truck."

With the ice and fresh water running into the pool, the temperature dropped to 92 by the time the guests arrived at one-thirty. Thank God a thunderstorm came at the same time.

It's a little more difficult maintaining control as a host when parties are away from home, but somehow I manage, even if it's a party given for me, as on my fiftieth birthday. That party was the three kinds of parties I hate most rolled into one. One, I was not the host; two, it was in a restaurant I had never been to before; and three, it was a surprise party. Of them all, I think I hate the surprise most. It seems like the dumbest thing to do to a middle-aged man or woman, having a bunch of people jump up in a darkened room and yell, "Surprise!" It's an open invitation to a heart attack.

I've always told Jeanette never to give me one. But when my fiftieth birthday was coming up, I suddenly smelled something in the air. For one thing, there were no plans for any party at all. I felt alternately suspicious and angry. Could it be that Jeanette would ignore such a milestone completely? Then I noticed little whispers and looks between her and Elainie and our close friends and neighbors. So I begged Jeanette, "Do not give me a surprise party. Please don't. I'll hate it."

My birthday came and went unnoticed. I figured Jeanette was punishing me. Then on Monday, a week later, I was having lunch at Maxwell's Plum and a few tables away was Steve Smith. As he left, he came over and said, "See you tomorrow night."

Tomorrow night, I thought? What's tomorrow night? Then it hit me. I ran after him and caught him at the checkroom. He already realized what he had done and started to apologize. I said, "Don't worry. I know all about the party, but don't tell Jeanette. By the way, do you really like that place?" He answered that he had never been there because he rarely gets down to Greenwich Village, but that he was looking forward to it because Mimi Sheraton had reviewed it a few weeks ago and it sounded like an interesting little French country restaurant.

I rushed back to my office and called the *Times* and asked about any review of a French country restaurant in the Village that had run in the last two or three weeks. Sure enough, they come up with La Metairie. I get into my car and tell Dave to drive to the address. He goes white. Of course he knew about the place because he had taken Jeanette there to make arrangements and he was afraid she would think he told me.

"What do you want to go there for, Mr. King?" he stammers. "It's probably closed now."

"Don't ad-lib. Just drive," I tell him.

I walk into the restaurant and it's between meals. No one is there except a few people in the kitchen. "I'd like to have a table for two for tomorrow night," I said. "Sorry, sir," was the answer. "We're closed for a private party tomorrow night."

I had noticed that right near the door there was a sort of buffet and I opened the top drawer and slipped my driver's license inside.

The next night Jeanette tells me we're seeing Steve Smith for dinner and she gives me the name and address of La Metairie. She was going to meet me there because, she said, she wanted to shop with Jean in the Village. The date was for eight and I showed up at eight-thirty. I walked in and everyone jumped up and yelled, "Surprise!" I never moved an eye. My expression never changed. I calmly said hello to everyone and Jeanette looks like she's ready to kill me.

She says, "You can't give anyone the satisfaction of surprising you, can you?"

I said, "What surprise? I knew about it all along."

"Come on, tell the truth," she said. "You didn't know about this party and it's a restaurant you've never been to before."

"I was here last night," I said.

"You're lying," she said.

"Look in that drawer," I told her.

She opened it and, of course, found my license. She never gave me a party again — surprise or otherwise.

Some of my favorite parties are those I have given away from home and even then I pay special attention to the menu. Only once have I been distracted from the food by a guest whose arrival seemed more important than the meal. It was a party I gave for Jeanette at the Villa Vera. We went there every winter for about fifteen years and always celebrated our anniversary there. We were talking about our twentieth anniversary in New York one night while we were with Frank Sinatra at Jilly's, the club owned by his buddy, Jilly Rizzo. Frank said, "Your twentieth? I'm coming down for that. Anyone who can stay married to this bum for twenty years deserves a special tribute." Jeanette was beside herself. She's been crazy about Sinatra since his Tommy Dorsey days.

I planned the party with Teddy Stauffer, who owned the Villa Vera and who was an outstanding host. Cocktails were served in his duplex apartment and dinner would be around the hotel pool, which was filled with flowers for the evening. There was a whole suckling pig spiced with garlic and chili peppers roasting on a spit and a lovely old Mexican woman patting handmade tortillas while another mashed avocados into guacamole in a big stone mortar. Everything was on schedule except for one thing. Not a word from Sinatra. By cocktail time, Jeanette was frantic.

"If he says he's coming, he's coming," I tried to assure her and myself at the same time. "He has a private plane and he'll be here. Stop bothering me. We have sixty other guests, many of them more famous than Frank."

"Name one," she said.

We started cocktails at six-thirty. Everyone looked wonderful in white pants, embroidered Mexican shirts, sandals, the works. The mariachi band was playing and all Jeanette kept mumbling was "Where's Frank? Where's Frank?"

All of a sudden the phone rang. It was Frank, calling from Ruby Dunes, one of his favorite hangouts in Palm Springs. "Alan, I'm stuck here with a lot of people. I just won't be able to get away. I tried to call you earlier," he said, "but you had already left your room. Let me explain to Jeanette."

Now I was really feeling low and as Jeanette listened to him, tears gathered in her eyes, even though she kept saying, "Yes, yes. Of course I understand, Frank. We're disappointed, but we understand."

Just as we were leaving the living room to go to the pool for dinner, the door to Stauffer's upstairs bedroom opens and out walks Frank. He yells, "Surprise!" I almost fainted. He had been up there all along and that's where he made the call. Even I started to cry. With him was a contingent of our Palm Springs friends.

After dinner we went to our favorite disco, Le Club, and by that time the *papparazzi* were all over us because the word was out that Frank was there. I felt responsible for his evening and really wanted him to have a good time. But there was one photographer I knew would be trouble. I couldn't get rid of him. We were all drunk and dancing with each other's wives and this guy comes sneaking around the tables. I walk over to him and say, "I'm gonna tell you this one more time. If you do not leave, I'm going to take that camera away from you. You're out of line. I just don't want you here."

Frank knows nothing about this but I keep watch and, sure enough, five minutes later I see this jerk behind a potted palm taking pictures. I grab his camera and smash it on the ground. This guy comes at me and I belt him. The place goes crazy and Sinatra clears right out, not wanting to be part of this scene. He gets to his plane with his gang at five-thirty in the morning, he flies away. Next morning, all the headlines read, "Frank Sinatra K.O.'s photographer."

I said to Jeanette, "I'll be a son of a bitch! This is the first time I had the guts to hit a photographer, and Frank gets all the credit."

There's one party I love to give because I can really go crazy with the food and not have to pay for it. It's the Roman orgy at the end of April at Caesars Palace in Las Vegas. The hotel picks up the tab. They invite one thousand high rollers and stuff them before the kill. It's held around the pool on the Saturday night before the Sunday finals of the Alan

King/Caesars Palace Tennis Classic and "orgy" is no idle term for it. It's complete with gladiators, real slave girls and real lions. The buffet supper for two thousand is so lavish that if Mark Antony saw the tab he'd say, "Friends! Romans! Countrymen! Separate checks!"

I hold long planning sessions with the very capable food and beverage managers, the chefs and waiters and the bartenders. It's like *Star Wars*. But the final results are worth it, with whole sides of beef being barbecued and grills where we do every kind of steak, lamb and veal chops, chickens, ribs, sausages, burgers and brochettes. The tables are loaded with salads and vegetables and breads as well as desserts.

For the finale, we have fireworks arranged by the maven George Plimpton. The first time he had planned the greatest display ever: an international display where in fifty minutes we would see firework styles typical of each country that specializes in them — India, China, Italy and so on. But we hadn't counted on the mistral, the hot dry wind that blows in from the desert. An hour before we were supposed to start, the fire department closed us down. They said with that wind and the amount of pyrotechnics we had, we could burn down the whole city. Did you ever see a grown man cry? Plimpton, I mean.

When I'm paying for the food myself, my tastes become much simpler, like the chili open house I give for the CBS crew at the U.S. Open in Flushing at the end of August. That's really my vacation. I blank out my calendar for those two weeks and from morning to night I breathe tennis. The high point for me is the chili lunch, and though it's for the sportscasters, players and officials, everyone comes.

I make the chili the day before at home and, as always, I use a leftover batch from the freezer as a starter. I combine olive oil and vegetable oils and use lots of beef and sausage with plenty of herbs and spices. I add cubed beef, too, because that gives me a rich thick sauce with plenty of chewy solids and I use both black and cayenne pepper so the sauce is hot all over the tongue. I make about four gallons and because they have only small electric warmers at the tournament grounds, I get it hot at home and carry it to Flushing with a big blanket wrapped around the pot. I set up at the CBS Control Center and before the chili I serve hot dogs stuck into hollowed-out French bread. Last year my cooking equipment blew all the electric lines and CBS went black for almost a minute.

Perhaps the tennis buffs among you remember two years ago when in the middle of a match with Ivan Lendl, Jimmy Connors ran off the court. Pat Summerall, John Newcombe and Tony Trabert in the CBS booth speculated on the reason for the sudden departure. Summerall thought that Connors was having trouble with his zipper. Trabert, remembering what once happened to him in his own tournament days, figured Connors' pants must have split. But John Newcombe guessed right, and when it was over, announced, "Alan King's chili has propelled Connors off the court and on to victory!"

When it comes right down to it, I feel that the best party I ever gave away from home was in Florida. I played a three-week engagement at Eden Roc, back in the fifties when Miami was one of the great entertainment centers. Friends had lavish parties every night and always invited Jeanette, to keep her entertained while I worked. When the engagement was over, I wanted to reciprocate by doing something special. How could I top what they had done for her?

Then I got an idea. I chartered a city bus with a regular uniformed driver and I had a bar set up in it and hired three violinists. I took thirty-six people on the longest, most involved progressive dinner in history — about seven courses in all, at different restaurants for the best dish at each. We started with cocktails and hors d'oeuvres on a friend's yacht and then went to Joe's Stone Crab for the first course and then to The Place for Steaks for their excellent beef, and so on. I planned it so there would be about fifteen to twenty minutes between stops and it lasted all night.

One of my guests was Nat Hiken, father of the situation comedy and the creator of Sergeant Bilko. As we were driving down Collins Avenue toward our last stop, Hiken turns to me and says, "Let's have some fun." He tells the driver, "Dim all the lights and pull up at the next bus stop." There's a woman waiting for a bus. The driver opens the door and she gets on. She's an attractive woman in her mid-fifties in a nurse's white uniform with her name, Ruth, on the nameplate over one pocket. Without noticing a thing, she drops her fare in the box and walks to a seat. As the bus rolls away, the bright lights come up, the violins begin to play and a couple starts dancing in the aisle. She looks up with a dazed look of total bewilderment.

"Would you like a drink?" I ask her.

She thinks for a minute, then asks, "Aren't you Alan King? What's going on?"

I tell her I was hired by the city to host a special party bus as a promotion for public transportation in Miami. Without batting an eye she says, "I'll have a scotch and soda." Finally I told her the truth, but by then she'd had three drinks and forgot about getting off. We took her to our last stop, a Greek joint noted for its baklava dessert and its belly dancers. We invited Ruth to come in with us, but she said she was tired, having been on her feet during the whole night shift at the hospital. We had the driver take her to her door.

Although that was long ago, I still have nightmares that somewhere in Florida there's a woman committed to an asylum because she told stories about an all-night party bus that cruised the streets of Miami with violins, a bar and Alan King as emcee.

 TURKEY WITH CRAZY EGGS

SERVES 10 TO 12

The eggs expand as the turkey roasts and take on a custardlike texture. Alan's kids named the stuffing "crazy eggs."

Singe and clean an 18-pound turkey. Rub insides with salt, pepper, a cut clove of garlic and softened butter. Discard garlic.

Heat 3 tablespoons butter in a skillet. When hot add 1 large, coarsely diced green pepper, 1 large, chopped onion and ½ cup coarsely chopped mushrooms. Sauté vegetables until soft but not brown. Stir in 12 very well-beaten eggs. Season with salt and pepper. Cook briefly, stirring constantly until eggs are slightly scrambled but still soft, almost as they would be for pipérade. Stir in 1½ cups seasoned poultry bread stuffing.

Preheat oven to 425 degrees. Fill turkey cavity with egg mixture and sew closed. Sprinkle outside of turkey with salt and pepper and rub with a generous amount of softened butter. Truss firmly.

Chop 2 carrots, 2 stalks of celery and 1 large onion and place them in the roasting pan. Place turkey on its side over the vegetables. Roast for about 20 minutes, or until golden brown. Turn to the other side and brown again. Then turn breast side up for another 20 minutes and when that has browned, reduce oven heat to 350 degrees.

Continue roasting until turkey is done — about 2 hours. Baste frequently with pan drippings. If butter in pan begins to burn, add chicken stock, 1 cup at a time. Turkey is done when drumsticks move freely in their sockets.

For gravy, pour all pan juices and vegetables through a strainer into a saucepan. Rub vegetables through as much as possible. To incorporate coagulated pan juices, add a little white wine to the roasting pan, bring to a boil and scrape browned bits loose with a wooden spatula. Add to strained pan juices. Let juices stand until fat rises, then skim. Serve turkey slices with a spoonful or two of the stuffing for each portion.

 ## BARBECUED SPARERIBS WITH HONEY GLAZE

SERVES 4 TO 6

For 3 racks of spareribs: place ribs on a rack in an open roasting pan. Cover bottom of pan with boiling water. Bake in preheated 375-degree oven for about 30 minutes, or until ribs begin to soften and look cooked. Turn ribs once during cooking.

Meanwhile prepare sauce. Heat 4 tablespoons olive oil in a large, heavy saucepan and sauté 1 large, finely minced onion and 3 cloves finely minced garlic until soft but not brown. Stir in 1 bottle chili sauce, 1 cup honey, ¼ cup Worcestershire sauce, 1 tablespoon powdered mustard, ¼ cup soy sauce and ½ cup wine vinegar. Stir until smooth. Add 2 bay leaves and generous sprinklings of dried thyme and oregano. Stir to blend, bring to a boil and simmer for about 40 minutes, stirring frequently. Check seasonings and adjust with salt, black pepper and more honey, soy sauce, vinegar or Worcestershire, as needed.

Drain water from rib pan after 30 minutes. Continue baking for 30 minutes. Then brush on barbecue sauce and bake ribs for an additional hour. Turn ribs and brush both sides with sauce as they bake.

Cut ribs apart and keep at room temperature until just before they are to be glazed over a barbecue grill. Reserve leftover sauce.

Ten minutes before they are to be served, brush ribs

with additional sauce and glaze over white-hot char-coal, turning so both sides of each rib brown. Serve im-mediately. Extra sauce can be passed separately. This makes four to six servings, depending on what else is served.

RACK OF LAMB PERSILLÉ

SERVES 6 GENEROUSLY

You will need 2 racks of lamb, each with about 7 or 8 chops. Butcher should saw through cross bone on top of chops. Let stand at room temperature 30 minutes be-fore roasting. Preheat oven to 425 degrees.

Sprinkle racks on all sides with salt and pepper. Stand, meat side up, in an open roasting pan. Roast for 15 minutes for rare meat, about 20 minutes for medium and 25 to 30 for well-done.

While lamb roasts, prepare a mixture of ⅔ cup fresh fine breadcrumbs, ¼ cup finely minced Italian parsley, 3 crushed garlic cloves and 3 tablespoons melted butter.

Remove lamb from oven and turn oven heat up to 500 degrees. Brush top of meat side with a very light coating of Dijon mustard.

Pack breadcrumb mixture firmly onto surface of lamb. Return lamb to upper half of the oven and roast at the higher heat for about 8 to 10 minutes, or until crumbs are faintly golden and crisp. Serve with sautéed zucchini.

To serve, cut into individual chops.

SAUTÉED ZUCCHINI

SERVES 6

Using the fine shredding blade of a food processor, grate 2 pounds (6 to 8) medium-size, washed zucchinis. Sprinkle with 1 tablespoon coarse salt. Place in colander and let juices drain out. That will take about 15 minutes. Squeeze handfuls of the zucchini to remove as much moisture as possible.

Heat 3 tablespoons butter in a large skillet. When foaming, add zucchini, breaking up clumps with a wooden spatula. Sauté, tossing almost constantly, for about 7 minutes, or until zucchini is wilted.

Sprinkle with salt, pepper, a tablespoonful of lemon juice and a big handful of minced parsley. Raise heat and toss zucchini for a minute or two. Serve immediately with rack of lamb.

U.S. OPEN CHILI

SERVES ABOUT 20

THIS IS HALF THE AMOUNT ALAN KING MAKES FOR THE TENNIS TOURNAMENT.

Heat ¼ cup olive oil in a heavy 12-inch skillet. In it, sauté 2 cups chopped onion, 2 tablespoons minced garlic and ¾ cup each diced red and green pepper. Stir over moderate heat until vegetables are wilted but not brown. Sprinkle with salt and pepper and turn into a heavy 8- to 9-quart pot or Dutch oven.

Heat ¼ cup light vegetable oil in the same skillet. Divide 5 pounds ground lean beef chuck in half. Brown each batch in the skillet, breaking up clumps of meat as it cooks. Sprinkle with salt and pepper and add to the pot.

Add 2 pounds Italian hot sausage meat (without casings) to the skillet and brown lightly, breaking up clumps. Add that to the pot.

Still in the same skillet, lightly brown in two batches 4 pounds cubed beef flank or skirt steak, adding oil to the skillet if needed. Set cubed beef aside in a bowl.

Add 3 large 1-pound 12-ounce cans of Italian plum tomatoes with their liquid to the pot and put it on the heat so that mixture begins to simmer as you add other ingredients. Stir in contents of one 12-ounce can of tomato paste. Add 1 tablespoon powdered cumin, 1 tablespoon ground black pepper, 1 tablespoon hot dried red pepper flakes, 2 tablespoons chili powder and the juice of ½ lemon. Add 3 tablespoons each dried oregano and thyme, rubbing them in between your palms. Add 4 bay leaves, stir to blend and add 1 or 2 small pork bones.

If you use dried red kidney beans, add 1½ pounds now. If you prefer canned beans, they will be added later.

Stir in 1 cup beef bouillon and bring mixture to a boil. Reduce heat and cook tightly covered at a slow, steady simmer for about 3 hours, or until mixture begins to thicken and meat becomes fairly soft. Add cubed beef. Continue cooking 3 more hours. Stir frequently during cooking and add bouillon or water if chili seems in danger of scorching. If you cannot lower heat enough to prevent scorching, place an asbestos mat or a Flame-Tamer under the pot.

If you use canned red kidney beans, drain them and rinse them under running cold water and add to the simmering chili. Three cans, each about 1 pound, will be the right amount. They should be added for the last hour of cooking.

Store cooked chili in the refrigerator for up to five days. To reheat, bring to a boil, reduce heat, and simmer for 1 hour, adding bouillon or seasonings as needed.

If you have leftover chili, freeze it and add it to a new batch made later. It gives it a richer, complex flavor, or so Alan King says. He also says this chili is best served with chopped raw onion and additional red pepper flakes. I prefer a topping of chopped scallions (green and white portions), a few drops of chili pepper vinegar and some steamed white rice. Neither of us thinks cheese has any place on this dish.

CHAPTER NINE

🌿 Cooking à la King

How does Alan King really cook? That was the question I kept asking myself since he first asked me for a roast chicken recipe. I wondered not only how well he cooked — how good his food was — but how adept he was at handling utensils, what kind of equipment he used, how he organized a cooking schedule for a complete dinner and whether he was messy or neat. What I wanted to see, in short, was "A Cooking Day in the Life of Alan King."

I suggested that he cook and let me watch. "What are you? A voyeur? I tell you what," he said, "you cook with me. We'll do a meal together at my house and invite guests to eat it." And so the plan got underway.

We based the menu on dishes he was sure of and did well. I added others that would make for a more or less unified meal. Throughout, there was a tacit understanding that we were trying for a bit of overkill so guests would have many things to taste. We were ten

*in all and among the guests was Gene Young, our editor
for this book, who, though she graciously refrained from
saying so, was beginning to doubt that there ever would
be a book. Eating, we thought, would be believing. The
guests' only qualifications, besides being friends, were
to have hearty appetites, adventurous palates and no
known allergies or predilections for foods that were
low-salt, low-sugar, low-cholesterol, low-calorie, or for
that matter, low anything. Our food would be high in
everything.*

 This was our menu:

APPETIZERS
Crabmeat Ray Stark (A.K.)
New Orleans Shrimp Rémoulade (M.S.)
Swedish Meatballs (M.S.)
Guacamole Dip with Crudités (A.K. and M.S.)

FIRST COURSE
*Fusilli with Frank Sinatra's New and Improved
Tomato Sauce (F.S. and A.K.)*

MAIN COURSES
Roast Parsley Chicken (A.K.)
*Braised Veal Shanks — Stinco de Vitello alla Missoni
(M.S.)*
Tai Missoni's Vegetable Casserole (M.S.)

DESSERTS
Phony Homemade Ice Cream (A.K.)
Cookies (Prime Concern Bakery)

 *And so on a cold, sunny Saturday morning in
mid-February, I drove out to Alan's home on Long Island Sound, carrying with me a huge red enameled
cast-iron Dutch oven, the veal shanks, and some fresh*

*herbs we thought might be unavailable in Great Neck.
"Be here by ten and don't be late!" Alan cautioned the
night before.*

*10:20 A.M. Sure enough, I am twenty minutes late,
a rare occurrence for me and one due to a zealous traffic
cop in the city who gave me a $45 ticket for making an
illegal turn. I can feel Alan's tension vibrating through
the half-timbered walls of the house.*

*Even so, I take a moment to enjoy the setting. Clear
white winter light silvers the cold blue waters of the
Sound, earth-toned ducks and wild geese squat on the
shore, sunning themselves, and remains of a recent
snowfall dust the lawns and trees. Seeing about eight
cars lining the graveled driveway, I think perhaps some
guests have arrived early, but I soon learn that all of the
cars belong to Alan, Jeanette and their daughter,
Elainie.*

*10:25. We unload my car and go into the kitchen.
Jeanette waits in a pale lavender workout suit, all set to
play tennis. We sit around the kitchen table to go over
the menu, plan the shopping trip and have coffee. Jeanette volunteers, "My specialty is buying things. I'll wait
in case there's anything you want me to pick up."*

*Three plump chickens covered with a thick layer of
butter and draped with bacon are already in a baking
pan.*

*10:35. Alan and I finish the menu, adding a gua-
camole dip here and a garnish of vegetables there.*

*"And we'll get big ripe strawberries for the ice
cream," he says.*

*"And don't forget prosciutto for the pasta sauce," I
add.*

We are both getting excited at the prospect of han-

dling so much food and are interrupting each other and almost shouting. Suddenly Jeanette, whom we had almost forgotten, slams her hand down on the table. "I don't believe what's going on here," she yells. "You're having an affair right in front of my eyes."

10:40. *I check out the refrigerator to see what staples are on hand. The top shelf is full of pastel tubes, bottles and jars, labeled "Avocado Mask," "Cucumber Lotion," "Buttermilk Freshener" and "Oatmeal Creme."*

"Maybe we don't need guacamole," I say. "We could make a dip out of these things." Turns out they were all Elainie's "natural" cosmetics. It occurs to me that someone should invent a beauty cream that could also be served on Ritz crackers.

10:45. *I announce that I can't find allspice.*

10:46. *Jeanette finds a jar of allspice.*

10:47. *Jeanette drops the jar in the sink and it smashes. Alan mumbles something, fortunately unintelligible.*

10:48. *I add allspice to the shopping list.*

10:50. *Alan shows me around the big yellow and white tiled kitchen with its dark wood paneling and terra-cotta floor, and huge double Garland restaurant range and all of the various work areas. I look in closets and drawers and find every utensil known to man. For good measure, we go down to the basement kitchen and storeroom and unearth more pots, serving platters and the wines. For the white that will accompany appetizers and the pasta, we choose a 1981 Meursault and for the red, a marvelously full-bodied, velvety St. Julien — a 1979 Château Beychevelle. Alan also takes out a magnum of Roederer Cristal champagne to have with dessert.*

11:05. *"First take a Maserati, Quatro Porte,"* Alan says as if it were the start of a recipe. It is a recent acquisition and a handsome and comfortable one at that. Our first stop is a Food Emporium supermarket with astonishingly wide aisles; I am accustomed to negotiating in tight-spaced Manhattan markets. Alan pushes the huge cart, bagging and weighing produce and struggling with packages that are so intricately stacked it is impossible to extricate one without toppling ten. As we progress, he explains that he and Jeanette always shop together for company. That way they get spontaneous ideas about food they see. They never telephone orders for parties. En route, Alan mistakes someone else's cart for his own and is halfway down the next aisle before realizing that the contents look unfamiliar. The Pablum was the tip-off.

Despite his noncelebrity outfit, which included a brimmed, Irish wool tweed walking hat, several customers come over to greet him. One young woman, obviously an employee, asks for an autograph.

11:30. Alan gets on the checkout line, choosing what looks like the shortest but moves the slowest. When he tells the clerk he wants to pay by check, she says, *"Do you have any identification?"* He looks up and it is the same girl who asked for his autograph.

"If you didn't know who I am, why did you want my autograph?" he demands. It takes ten minutes to get the O.K.

12:05. Back to the Maserati after a small confrontation with a shopping cart that keeps rolling downhill as we unload it. Then on to the seafood store, the Italian salumeria for fresh pasta and cheese, back to a small shop for lemons and watercress, which we forgot, yet another stop for prosciutto and finally to the bakery *for cookies. Throughout the odyssey, Alan keeps asking, "What are we going to have for lunch?" I say there will be enough to nibble on as we go along.*

12:50. We return from shopping ten minutes ahead of schedule. I put on cooking clothes, Jeanette leaves for her game. With the help of the housekeeper, Gussie, all of the purchases are unpacked and sorted. I notice Alan busy in the breakfast corner, laying place-mats, slicing salami, pilfering pieces of the prosciutto and cutting bread and cheese. He opens the Creole mustard I had brought for the rémoulade sauce and begins eating it with a spoon, like a relish. Intermittently he munches on half-sour pickles, and sips beer. Lunch is served.

1:15. We begin to cook, each going about our routines and miraculously not bumping into each other once, a testimonial to the layout of this spacious kitchen with its two sinks and four chopping centers. As I prepare my recipes, I keep an eye on Alan. Dressed in a plaid cotton shirt, jeans, moccasins and wearing a full no-nonsense denim apron, he is most businesslike as he picks over the crabmeat. He is a very tidy and contained worker and almost completely professional with a French chef's knife although he holds the blade with two hands and chops back and forth, rather than holding the handle in one hand, and rocking the blade back and forth against the palm of the other. I try to correct him by saying, "André Soltner does it this way."

"André Soltner doesn't tell jokes," he answers, not following the method of Lutèce's owner-chef.

1:45. Alan starts to whip cream for the ice cream. "How the hell do you turn this mixer on?" he asks. I do it for him, wondering, but forgetting to ask, how he has

*turned it on before. Gadgets and mechanical equipment
seem to intimidate him. "Oh, great" was his reply when
I said that I would not need the food processor.*

2:30. *For the fifth time, Alan massages his
chickens, removing the strips of bacon, slipping out the
parsley crammed into their interiors and working the
butter over them, inside and out. Each time he has a
strange faraway look in his eye. Maybe it is better than
sex. I wonder if he will have the heart to put them in the
oven when the time comes.*

*"I don't have to truss these, do I?" he asks at one
point and is relieved when I say no. A man who cooks
with enormous energy, he has little patience with intricate handwork, a characteristic I share. "I only began
roasting a few years ago," he tells me. "I'm basically a
sauté man. I like all the food out in the open so I can see
what's happening to it."*

*"Do you think we have enough?" we keep asking
each other all during the day. Would two pounds of
pasta really be enough for twelve? Should we get more?
Would three chickens and five shanks of veal allow for
seconds? Typically we count on full portions of each
dish on the menu, as though there were not a dozen to
be tasted.*

3:00. *He tastes my rémoulade sauce and pro-
nounces it perfect. Not so my guacamole. He thinks it
needs more salt because it will be eaten with raw vegetables. I do not agree and add none.*

*I prefer the crabmeat Ray Stark without horserad-
ish, but don't want to hurt his feelings. He explains as
he makes that dish that it was the invention of Walter,
the maître d' at "21," who did it as a variation on crabmeat Remick for the producer Ray Stark. I tell him*

about the origins of the veal shank and vegetable casserole recipes. Both had been served to me at a wonderful dinner given by the fashion designers Rosita and
Tai Missoni in their home outside of Milan.

3:20. By now, Gussie has a very able and pleasant
helper, Helen, who busily chops and slices vegetables
and peels shrimp. But like Gussie and Jeanette, Helen
proves to be an overzealous cleaner.

"Stop cleaning," I finally say as she pulls a just-
used spatula out of my hand to wash it and hide it.

"That's what he says," she answers with a laugh.

We both lose our tempers slightly when Helen or
Gussie stands at the stove with a damp cloth, wiping up
droplets that fall as we baste.

3:45. "Where is the goddam extension cord for the
hot plate?" Alan yells. The cleaners had been at it
again.

The only other frustration is that all utensils are
stored out of sight in closets and drawers. Being of the
let-it-all-hang-out school of kitchen design, I like spatu-
las, spoons, knives and the like to be right where I can
get my hands on them instantly. Bogged down with a
huge, hot, cast-iron casserole full of veal shanks that
needed turning, I do not enjoy having to open a door,
slide out a panel and unhook the turning fork.

"That's Jeanette's contribution to the design of
this kitchen," Alan explains. "She doesn't want it to
look as though anyone ever cooks here."

4:00. Alan prepares his Mornay sauce, working
skillfully with a wire whisk, turning it in and out of
corners to keep lumps out of the cream sauce and beating constantly. But unlike professional chefs who use
only a wrist motion, he uses his whole body and keeps

bouncing on the balls of his feet as though he is ready to return a tennis serve. Again I invoke Soltner's name. "Screw André Soltner. Can he make matzo brei?" he asks.

4:20. Jeanette returns, ready to hold forth in her domain — table-setting.

"What silver will you need?" she asks.

"Well, we're going to have the pasta when we first sit down," Alan begins, "and then guests will go to the buffet for the main course —"

Jeanette interrupts: "I don't want to hear about the food. Just tell me exactly what pieces of silver and which plates you will need."

When she is done, the table in the elegant country dining room looks superb — long graceful red and white flowers in cut-crystal vases, single candles in delicate glass holders placed intermittently down the length of the table and hand-crocheted Portuguese placemats that look like white sugar frosting. Flower-sprigged fluted dishes and gilded flatware add a warm, springtime touch. Jeanette also places a flower and fresh towels in each guest bathroom and clears hangers in the hall closet.

5:15. The veal shanks are braised golden brown, the vegetables are mellowing in the oven and Alan finally parted with his chickens, now turning a glorious copper golden brown. There is time to rest, shower and dress and to soothe feet that are beginning to feel the effects of a hard tile floor.

6:30. An hour before the guests are expected, we return to the kitchen and arrange as much food as possible. I slice the veal, put it back in its pot and cover it with pan juices and a lid to keep it warm. Alan slides his darling chickens to the back of the range so they won't catch a chill. Appetizers are turned into serving dishes and we rehearse the placement of platters on the buffet.

7:30. The first guests arrive and walk through the kitchen on their way to the guest house, where appetizers will be served. They look in pots, nibble and pronounce everything perfect. Alan likes guests to go through the kitchen to raise their expectations.

8:00. Most guests are assembled and eating and drinking begin. Only a few are late.

9:00. Guests help themselves to main courses from the buffet and gather at the dinner table. "Ooohs" and "aahs" are abundant. Steve and Renée Levy, two of Alan's best eater friends, agree that this food is better than anything they get in most restaurants. They are right, of course.

9:45. My critical faculties take over. How would I rate the meal? Appetizers were for the most part excellent; flaws were the insufficient browning of the meatballs and the slightly zapping dose of horseradish in the crab. Raw vegetables would perhaps be more pleasant to chew if lightly blanched, then chilled. The pasta and roast chicken are as good as they can get. So is the veal, but because of the large center bone in each slice (as in osso buco), the portions look discouragingly large to several of the women, especially with other dishes to be tasted. Nothing to do about that but let them take partial slices, or invite guests with lustier appetites. The vegetable casserole tastes as beautiful as it looks. The dessert is luscious, but would be better without chocolate, and perhaps the strawberries would look more interesting streaked rather than blended through the mass of ice cream.

Three out of a possible four stars seems like the
right rating, considering exquisite service and ambience.
10:30. Coffee is poured. I secretly slip my shoes off,
as my feet are in agony. Alan and Jilly Rizzo are talk-
ing about Harry Belafonte and old times during the
Selma march and the civil rights movement to others at
their end of the table. Gradually, almost imperceptibly,
Alan's voice gets a little louder and guests farther down
the table turn toward him, listening. Finally all atten-
tion is fixed on him and he stands up. Alan King is on,
performing exactly as he does on stage and everyone
forgets the time. Alan forgets the Roederer Cristal.
(Later he says he did not forget. He didn't want to in-
terrupt himself.)
12:00. Most guests leave. A few stay behind to see a
movie Alan has borrowed for the evening.
Four days later. Alan and I have recovered from
what may have been one of history's biggest charley
horses — he in the Jacuzzi, I in a bubble bath. I call to
discuss details of the dinner and Jeanette gets on to say
how much they are enjoying leftovers — still.

CRABMEAT RAY STARK

SERVES 10 TO 12

Pick over 2 pounds of fresh lump crabmeat, to re-
move slivers of cartilage. Sprinkle with strained juice of
1 lemon. Remove leaves from ½ bunch of watercress
and chop. Add to crabmeat, along with 3 heaping table-
spoons of drained, bottled white horseradish.
Combine ¼ cup bottled chili sauce with ½ cup
mayonnaise. Add to crabmeat mixture. Season with salt
and freshly ground black pepper. Toss gently with a
fork so you do not mash crabmeat. If you want to pre-

pare this an hour or two in advance, keep crabmeat mixture in refrigerator and heat before final preparation.

Place mixture in a heavy saucepan and heat gently for a few minutes until crabmeat is quite warm but not hot. Stir constantly.

Make a Mornay sauce, using 4 tablespoons butter, 3 tablespoons flour and 2 cups hot, scalded half-and-half (milk and cream). Remove from heat and rapidly beat in 2 well-beaten egg yolks. Stir in 2 tablespoons each grated Gruyère and Parmesan cheeses. Season with salt and a generous amount of cayenne pepper. If you are preparing sauce an hour or two before it is to be served, spread a little butter on top so it will not form a film.

Thirty minutes before serving time preheat oven to 375 degrees. Divide crabmeat mixture among 10 to 12 small, lightly buttered ramekins or spread in large, buttered clam shells. Top each with 2 tablespoons Mornay sauce. For easy handling, set ramekins or clam shells in a large baking pan and place in upper third of preheated oven. Bake 15 to 20 minutes, or until sauce is bubbling and top is golden brown. Serve immediately.

Alan still thinks this should have horseradish. I say leave it out, but stir a teaspoonful of Dijon mustard into the sauce. More subtle.

❧ NEW ORLEANS SHRIMP RÉMOULADE

SERVES 6 TO 8

Buy 2 pounds of fresh shrimp that run about 25 to the pound. Place in large saucepan and cover with *water. Add 1 small, thinly sliced onion and a sliced stalk of celery with leaves, as well as a pinch of salt and 8 to 10 black peppercorns. Cover and slowly bring water to a full boil. Keep covered, turn off heat and let shrimp stand about 7 minutes. Drain at once and cool under running cold water. Drain, peel, devein and place in refrigerator until just before serving time.*

The sauce develops its flavor best if it matures in the refrigerator for about 3 hours before it is served. To make the sauce, use a blender, if you have one. A food processor will do, but the blender is more efficient with this amount of sauce. Place in the blender jar ¼ cup Creole mustard, 2 tablespoons hot Dijon-style mustard, 3 tablespoons sweet paprika, ¼ cup red wine vinegar, juice of ½ lemon and 1 cup olive oil. Blend for a second or two until combined.

To this add a generous pinch of cayenne pepper, 1 teaspoon salt, 1 cup chopped scallions (white and green portions), ½ cup chopped parsley leaves, ½ cup chopped celery, 1 clove garlic and 1 teaspoon minced fresh tarragon. Blend at high speed for 2 or 3 minutes, or until smooth. Taste and adjust seasonings, adding more of whatever is needed to produce a bright coral, highly spiced sauce that is the consistency of beaten sour cream.

Ten or 15 minutes before serving, stir sauce gently into shrimp and let sit at room temperature. If it is to be served buffet-style, turn into a large glass bowl with a serving spoon. If it is to be served individually at the table, line 8 salad plates with shredded romaine lettuce or with leaves of Boston lettuce. Spoon shrimp and sauce over and serve.

NOTE: If you cannot get fresh tarragon, use tarragon vinegar instead of the red wine vinegar.

🌿 SWEDISH MEATBALLS

SERVES 12 TO 18

You will need 2½ pounds of meat that can be half beef and half veal, or 1 pound each beef chuck and lean pork, plus ½ pound of lean veal, the latter being my preference. These meats should be finely ground. Ask the butcher to grind them together so they will be well mixed.

Soak 1 cup breadcrumbs in 1½ cups half-and-half (milk and cream) until all liquid is absorbed. Sauté 1 finely minced onion in 4 tablespoons butter until soft but not brown. Lightly beat 2 eggs.

Add the soaked breadcrumbs, sautéed onion and eggs to meat, with all pan butter. Season with about 1 teaspoon salt, ½ teaspoon black pepper and ½ teaspoon allspice. Mix everything together thoroughly. Your hands are best for this.

If mixture contains pork, do not taste raw to check seasonings. Instead, make a tiny patty and fry it, then taste and adjust. If there is no pork, you can taste the mixture raw. Add salt, pepper and allspice to taste.

Wet the palms of your hands with cold water and shape mixture into balls, each about 1 inch in diameter. Heat 3 tablespoons butter in a large skillet and begin browning meatballs. Do not crowd them into the pan or they will not brown. Do this in shifts, using 1 or 2 skillets and turning gently with a wooden spatula until brown on all sides. Scrape pan and add butter each time you remove meatballs. Reserve scrapings and drippings.

When all meatballs are brown, return all drippings to one pan. Sprinkle in 2 tablespoons of flour and stir over low heat for about 5 minutes, until absorbed. Pour in 1 cup hot, scalded milk and bring to a boil, stirring constantly with a whisk. Slowly add an additional cup of scalded milk to make thin gravy. Season with salt, pepper and allspice.

Return meatballs to pan and turn them very gently through the sauce. Serve at once or turn off heat and let stand until just before serving time, and then reheat, adding ¼ to ½ cup heavy cream, for 2 or 3 minutes.

This makes twelve to eighteen servings, depending on what else you are having.

NOTE: Usually these meatballs are made with pork in the meat mixture, but for our dinner we eliminated it because several guests preferred not to eat it.

GUACAMOLE DIP FOR CRUDITÉS

Mash two large, thoroughly ripe avocados (preferably Hass) with a stainless-steel fork in a glass, ceramic or stainless-steel bowl. Do not use silver, aluminum or plain steel utensils. Sprinkle immediately with juice of ½ lemon and mix through. Add half a grated onion, 1 small clove crushed garlic and several generous dashes of Tabasco sauce. Season to taste with salt (about ½ teaspoon should do).

Turn into a small glass, ceramic or stainless-steel bowl and imbed one avocado pit in the middle of the mixture to prevent blackening. This can be prepared an hour before serving.

Adjust seasonings and turn into serving bowl so vegetables can be dipped into it. Cucumbers cut in thin slivers, celery, scallions and green or sweet red peppers are the best vegetables to use. Raw mushrooms, carrots, broccoli and zucchini tend to overpower the flavor of the avocado. Alan thinks this needs more salt. He's wrong!

NOTE: *If guacamole is not to be used as a dip for vegetables, substitute 1 seeded, finely minced fresh jalapeño pepper for Tabasco sauce.*

FUSILLI WITH FRANK SINATRA'S NEW AND IMPROVED TOMATO SAUCE

Alan looked over the recipe for tomato sauce sent to him by Frank Sinatra and said, "What does an Italian know about spaghetti sauce? I'll have to doctor this up." He doubled the original recipe (page 93) and made the following changes: Tomatoes were drained and coarsely chopped, not blended. Their canning liquid was kept aside and added as the sauce thickened during cooking. Onions were cut in thick, rather than thin, crescents. They were simmered in the oil, along with sliced garlic, which was not removed, and ¼ pound chopped prosciutto. Fresh basil was used.

The sauce was served over 2 pounds of fusilli, the corkscrew pasta. It had been cooked in rapidly boiling, well-salted water and was drained and tossed with butter before being topped with the sauce.

This amount made 10 servings because we had so many other dishes. Normally it would make 6 to 8 appetizer portions.

🌿 ROAST PARSLEY CHICKEN

For each 3½-pound chicken:
Rub inside cavity with salt, black pepper and 1 tablespoon softened butter. Place two peeled cloves of garlic in the cavity and cram it with a handful of washed and dried Italian parsley, using both leaves and stems. Sprinkle outside of chicken with salt and pepper and rub all over generously and lovingly with softened, unsalted butter. Trussing is desirable but not necessary. It is also not necessary to keep massaging it with the butter unless you share Alan King's mishagos in doing so. Place chicken breast side down in an open roasting pan. Drape two slices of lean bacon over top.

Preheat oven to 400 degrees. Peel one small onion and cut into chunks. Scrape one carrot and cut into 3 or 4 pieces. Wash one stalk of celery with leaves and cut into 2 or 3 pieces. Add all vegetables and two peeled garlic cloves to the pan, placing them around the chicken.

Roast chicken breast side down for about 20 to 30 minutes or until skin begins to turn golden brown. Baste with pan juices several times.

Reduce oven heat to 350 degrees. Turn chicken breast side up and replace bacon strips on top. Pour ½ cup white wine in pan and use this for basting. Continue roasting and basting until chicken is done — about 1 hour more. Drumsticks should move easily and juices should run clear when thigh is pierced with a fork.

To serve, cut chicken into quarters, discarding

garlic and parsley. Separate wings from breasts and drumsticks from thighs. Spoon some of the reduced pan juice over cut pieces. If juice is too thin, bring to boil in a saucepan and reduce over high heat. Vegetables may be served or discarded, or, as is probable, eaten by the cook.

To make 2 to 3 chickens, proceed as above but line them all up in a large open roasting pan. Double the amount of vegetables and wine. The roasting time will be the same.

 ## STINCO DI VITELLO ALLA MISSONI

The shin or shank of the veal is the section from which osso buco is cut. But unlike that Italian specialty, in this recipe the shank is cooked whole, only partly slashed through the bone. It is then tied and braised as a roast. For 10 to 12 guests at a meal with many courses, 4 shanks will do. I used 5 because some of the end cuts are less attractive than mid-cuts.

Have the butcher saw through the bone of each shin, dividing it in four equal parts, each about 1½ inches thick. If the shank is long and 4 slices seem too thick, have it cut in 5 sections. But be sure the cut does not go through the flesh on the underside. The shank should be firmly tied with a string around each slice and from front to back, as for a shoulder roast or a sausage.

Remove meat from refrigerator about 30 minutes before cooking. Sprinkle each shank on all sides with salt and pepper and tuck tiny sprigs of fresh rosemary intermittently through the cord on both sides. There should be 8 to 10 sprigs in all.

For this number of shanks you will probably have to use 2 large Dutch ovens, preferably of enameled cast iron or flameproof earthenware. Into each pour a thin film of olive oil and heat until it shimmers.

Preheat oven to 325 degrees. Brown shanks in hot oil one at a time, turning to brown all sides and edges. Remove and keep warm. Continue until all shanks are brown, being careful not to burn oil and adding more if needed.

Return all of the browned shanks to the Dutch ovens. They should not be crowded in, but should fit fairly close.

Into each casserole pour ⅔ cup dry white wine and add 1 peeled clove of garlic cut in half lengthwise. Bring to a rapid boil and reduce until liquid is thick and has a golden, satiny sheen. Cover casseroles and place in middle of preheated oven.

Let meat braise slowly but steadily until tender. Turn it several times and add a little hot water if there is no liquid in pot. This will take about 1 hour. Do not let the veal cook until it falls apart. The bone should still be in place but tines of a long fork should slip in and out easily. Remove from oven and let stand covered in a warm place for 15 minutes before carving. To carve, remove strings and cut through sections.

Raise heat under pan juices and stir in any solids, adding a little hot water to deglaze sides if needed. If juices are too thin, reduce over high heat. Spoon a little pan juice over each slice and serve.

It is possible to slice meat an hour before serving

and return to pan juices, keeping all covered to stay hot. Reheat on top of stove in pan juices.

NOTE: *If you cannot get fresh rosemary, use a generous pinch of dried in each casserole, but add it after the meat has browned and you have reduced the wine.*

TAI MISSONI'S VEGETABLE CASSEROLE

To make this casserole you will need a large baking dish, preferably glass, so vegetables can be seen. The second choice is ceramic or porcelain. The pan should be about 12 x 16 inches for this amount of vegetables, which just served 10.

Before assembling casserole, prepare all vegetables. Peel 4 pounds of old boiling potatoes and slice very thinly and uniformly, as for scalloped potatoes. Keep slices in ice water so they won't turn color. It is best to use a stainless-steel knife for the slicing.

Wash and dry 2 small, very ripe eggplants. Do not peel. Cut in eighths lengthwise, then slice thinly. Every piece will then have an edge of skin. Wash and dry 4 zucchinis, cut them in half lengthwise and slice about ¼ inch thick. Slice 2 small green peppers and 2 small red peppers in thin rounds, then cut each round slice in half. Be sure to discard seeds. Peel 1 medium or 2 small red onions and slice thinly into half rounds. Slice 4 medium-size ripe tomatoes. Pit ½ to ⅔ cup of small black Nice or Gaeta olives. Do not worry about breaking them up.

This casserole takes about 2 hours to bake, so plan

*accordingly. It can be held for about 30 minutes in a
warm but turned-off oven.*

*Preheat oven to 375 degrees. Spread a small
amount of olive oil on the bottom of baking pan. Drain
potatoes and dry on a towel, then add to pan, spreading
in an even layer. Sprinkle lightly with salt, pepper and
a little olive oil.*

*Now add the other vegetables, forming stripes: at
each end, place several tightly packed rows of eggplant,
skin side up. Add two rows of zucchini next, then red
and green peppers, tomatoes (all skin side up) and red
onions. The order is not important as long as colors are
mixed. Vegetables can be packed closely, as they will
shrink in cooking.*

*Distribute olives over top of vegetables and gently
press down with your palms. Sprinkle with salt, pepper
and 3 to 4 tablespoons light olive oil. Cover pan with a
sheet of heavy-duty aluminum foil, or a double thickness of standard foil. Place in oven and bake.*

*Remove foil when vegetables begin to soften and
juices rise and bubble in the pan — about 40 minutes.
If vegetables become dry after they have been uncovered,
baste with juices and re-cover. Serve directly from pan,
using a spatula that will get down to the bottom of the
pan to pick up the potatoes, and that will hold juices.*

PHONY HOMEMADE ICE CREAM

SERVES 12

*The best ice cream to use for this is one that has a
high overrun, meaning it is airy.*

Let 1 quart vanilla ice cream soften at room tem-

perature until it can be easily spooned but is not yet liquid. Whip 1 ½ cups heavy sweet cream (preferably not ultra-pasteurized). Wash and hull 1 ½ pints ripe strawberries and puree in a blender, along with 3 tablespoons quick-dissolving granulated sugar.

Fold whipped cream and strawberries into ice cream. Fill two 10-inch ring molds to 1 inch of the rims with the mixture.

Smooth tops, cover with waxed paper, then with heavy-duty aluminum foil, and place in freezer for 5 to 7 hours. This can even be done the day before.

To unmold, run a thin knife blade around the edges of the ice cream in each mold. Then rub sides and bottom of mold with a cloth wrung out in very hot water. Place serving platter over mold and invert. Pray that ice cream slips out easily.

Fill ring with sliced strawberries and chunks of oranges that have been lightly sugared and macerated for 30 minutes in Grand Marnier or Fraises des Bois liqueur. Cut ice cream in sections and spoon fruit sauce over each portion.

For a light dessert, prepare fruit sauce of strawberries and oranges as described above. Allow ½ large orange and 5 to 6 strawberries for each guest.

CHAPTER TEN

 Have I Got a

Restaurant for You!

*This is the only chapter in this book where a
disclaimer is in order: the opinions on restaurants ex-
pressed in the following pages are strictly Alan King's
and do not necessarily reflect mine. We agree on all but
a small group of celebrity haunts that cater to those
who want to be with their colleagues and relax out of
the public eye. Non-celebrities do not require those conditions, and it is pointless for them to go to such places,
since the food and service will be indifferent and they
usually will not be seated within staring distance of the
heavy hitters.*

*Alan King explains his abiding affection for these
places very clearly: "They are my clubs. My people are
there. Civilians need not apply. If I've been away from
New York for more than a week, all I have to do to catch
up on what's happened in my business is to have a
drink or supper at '21,' lunch at the Russian Tea Room
and dinner at Elaine's. The Tea Room is like a Polish*

wedding. You can go from one table to another and pick up on all the conversations. I eat lightly there because I'm always saving myself for dinner. I like the chicken salad, the borscht with piroshky and, when they are on the menu, the Siberian pilmeny.

"But Elaine's is the most amazing restaurant in the world because of the people she attracts. I do more business there in three hours than I do during three days in California. Also, I hate to eat alone and if I walk in by myself after some function, Elaine sits with me and she's good company. I never eat at those banquets so I have some ziti with tomato sauce and ricotta and relax."

Because his dinner means so much to him, Alan King does not like to take chances with things going wrong. Usually he can get the table and attention he wants simply by using his own name when he makes a reservation. But he doesn't rely on that alone where he isn't known. During the course of our work on this book, he did go to several restaurants that he had never been to before, but only after I made the reservations. He will also go for the "first time" if a regular at the restaurant takes him and introduces him to the management. And if Alan King feels he isn't going to command special service in Paris, for example, he asks Giselle Masson of La Grenouille to call for him. She did that recently for Jamin, perhaps the hottest three-star restaurant in Paris, and Alan reported a thoroughly delightful experience. Once before, Madame Masson made a reservation for him at Lasserre in her name, saying that it was for a famous comedian. "We were treated magnificently," Alan said. "Then I caught a glimpse of the reservation book. They had written in 'Bob Hope.'"

There was a revealing occurrence also as our work on this book progressed. Jeanette and Alan took their first trip to Japan. I gave him the names of a few small, special restaurants I knew there many years ago, thinking he would never use them. But he came back with glowing reports of his meals at Okahan, known for its butter-yaki made with Matsuzaka beef, and Toricho, a tiny counter restaurant featuring yakitori — bits of chicken grilled on skewers. He reported on these forays with much pride. Then I had a report from Jeanette.

"We loved your restaurants in Japan," she said. "Of course Alan wanted to eat in our hotel. He's never been crazy about Japanese food. But I said I wanted to go to the restaurants on Mimi's list."

Could it be that Jeanette really has been taking a bum rap? Could she be the adventurous eater in the family? Will she and I write a book together called "Is Tofu Better Than Sex?" Stay tuned.

I APPRECIATE GOOD FOOD WHEREVER I find it, and a great dinner in someone's home is always a special pleasure. But to me, the ultimate dining experience has to be in a restaurant. The restaurant is the theater of the palate. I try to leave my office about an hour early for a dinner date so I have time to drop in at several restaurants along the way and get an idea of what's being featured around town that night.

Because a good restaurant is my reward for the day, I don't like surprises. I want an atmosphere I can be comfortable in. That doesn't always mean fancy. I am as comfortable at Elaine's, which is really a simple tavern, as I am at the elegant La Grenouille.

I had a streak of insanity long before the rest of the country developed restaurant madness. Let me explain how I got this way. To anyone who grew up poor during the Depression, restaurants were unattainable. It was considered a sin to spend three times more for food than it would cost at home. Because we couldn't afford it, my mother dismissed the whole idea by saying, "You never know what they're giving you in those places." All of that made restaurants seem like the ultimate luxury. And with the hectic conditions that prevailed at my mother's table, the idea of having a choice of dishes and being served in a calm and orderly way seemed miraculous. But nowadays with the overcrowded, noisy and trendy eating places, my mother's meals are beginning to seem restful by comparison.

We lived close to Peter Luger's steak house in Williamsburg and in those days all the bankers would come across the bridge for lunch. They rolled up in their Rolls-Royces and La Salles and Packard touring cars, like creatures from another world, which they were. I used to look into the windows to watch them eat. There was J. P. Morgan, John D. Rockefeller, Commodore Vanderbilt and Diamond Jim Brady — or so it seemed to me. Wall Street was only fifteen minutes away, but I figured it would take a lifetime to get there.

It was my Uncle Hymie who opened my eyes

by taking me to my first really formal, fine restaurant — Lundy's in Sheepshead Bay in Brooklyn. I was impressed by the white linens, the formality of the black waiters and the food — clams, chowders, biscuits and lobsters — all of that great seafood.

On my own, the only place I could afford was a neighborhood Chinese restaurant where I ordered one from column A, one from Column B. A complete meal cost forty cents. My mother said it was cheap because they used alley cats instead of chicken. Even so, it was the most exotic food I'd ever eaten. It was the first place I ever took Jeanette. When I told her where we were going, she said, "I hear they use alley cats instead of chicken." Her mother knew as much about restaurants as my mother. Every once in a while I still get a longing for that soft kind of Cantonese food with all the celery and bean sprouts in the chow mein and I can still get it at Lum's in Flushing.

When I began in show business as a boy, I spent a lot of time around Times Square, then a pretty raffish place. When I was broke I ate at Kellogg's cafeteria, where the comics hung out. We would sit there until four in the morning drinking coffee and telling lies. It was exactly like the opening scene in Woody Allen's *Broadway Danny Rose*.

I also went to the Horn & Hardart Automat on Broadway for the sandwiches and meat loaf and macaroni with cheese. But I had a special scam there. For my first portion, I'd put the coins in the slot and the little glass door would pop open so I could take out the sandwich. But before the door slammed shut, I stuck in a matchbook cover. The door would close and a replacement sandwich would be put in the compartment. I could then open the door without using more coins and take the second sandwich.

My biggest thrill was looking into the famous restaurants around Times Square. What excitement to see Jack Dempsey at the window table in his restaurant and to look into Lindy's and see Walter Winchell, Damon Runyon and Milton Berle! And I would go in for a drink at Dinty Moore's, just so I could watch Billy Rose and Rodgers and Hammerstein. It was an even bigger thrill to eventually be able to afford those places. They lived up to my expectations in every way. Lindy's chicken in the pot and its calf's liver were perfect, but I always preferred cheesecake at the Turf. Dinty Moore's had delicious whole little roast chickens served in individual casseroles and its corned beef and cabbage made every day St. Patrick's Day. Dinty's also made the best cole slaw I ever ate.

The only thing better than the pastrami sandwiches at the Stage Deli was a conversation with Max Asnes, the owner. He was a warm and generous man and would carry a broken-down actor on his books for months. If a customer complained that the corned beef was fatty, Max would pick up a slice in his hand, dash over to the counter and scream to his brother-in-law, the sandwich man, "If a customer wants lean, he should get lean." With that he'd throw the slice at his brother-in-law.

Fred Allen came in one day when Max was throwing a corned-beef fit and Fred said, "Hello, Max." No answer. "Hello, Max," he repeated. No answer. "Max," Fred called, "I've said hello to you twice."

"Awright . . . hello and a half," Max answered.

These days I go to the Carnegie Deli so I can still get the best corned beef and pastrami. But I really miss all of that food and history. What I miss most of all is Broadway.

I gradually became interested in the other side of New York eating and I began to try some of the great French and Italian restaurants. After all, it's possible to appreciate both good jazz and Mozart. It didn't take much for me to get used to the wonderful food at Café Chambord and later at Chauveron. They were both owned by Roger Chauveron, who served a marvelous cassoulet and some of the best duck and game pâtés I've ever had. I enjoyed a lot of simple neighborhood Italian restaurants, of course, but the first classy one I knew was Romeo Salta's. I met him when he started Chianti in Hollywood, but he got better at his New York place — the greatest pasta, the slices of filet mignon covered with pizzaiola sauce and roast peppers, the incredible zabaglione, for which Romeo used the egg shell to measure the Marsala — thick, foamy with just enough sugar and wine. Romeo, Romeo, wherefore art thou?

Working at Leon & Eddie's, I was next door to "21," but I never went in because I was a kid. I was finally introduced by the owner, Eddie Davis. Between shows, he would eat in the "21" kitchen with Mack Kriendler. They were so nice to me that they let me watch.

It was Maurice Chevalier who introduced me to the ultimate in French cooking. It was late on a Saturday, after we had been rehearsing together for the Ed Sullivan show and the buffet supper was set up for the cast.

"Can I get you something?" I asked Chevalier.

"Yes," he said, casing the table. "A taxi. I never eat when I can dine."

That was my introduction to Le Pavillon. It was a real turning point for me. The minute I entered I knew this was a whole different act. Haute cuisine, like other places I'd been to, but with a special kind of direction. The air vibrated with it. Chevalier told me about the owner, Henri Soulé, who had come to New York to run the restaurant at the French exhibition during the 1939 World's Fair and who stayed to change the style of French cooking in America. After that, I became a regular until Soulé died in 1966. To be taken to Le Pavillon by Maurice Chevalier is like being taken to the Museum of Modern Art by Picasso.

Whenever I had a date there, I'd arrive early and watch the last-minute preparations. It was like backstage just before the curtain goes up. I can still see Soulé running around barking orders, changing flowers, squeezing rolls to be sure they were fresh. Once I saw him reprimand a captain for having a pencil sticking out of his breast pocket. "You are a captain at Pavillon, not a bookkeeper," he said. He was a real tyrant, but I think that's what it takes. If I'm going into battle, I want Patton for a general, not Eisenhower. Ah, the memories of that incomparable lobster bisque, the quenelles and the chicken with champagne sauce, and for lunch in summer, the cold beef in aspic with tarragon, served with a salad of the tiniest haricots verts.

I was so grateful to Chevalier that I had to reciprocate. I took him to the Lower East Side and the old Parkway, where he relished the chicken fat, unborn eggs, mushroom and barley soup, kasha varnishkes, and the worst accordion player in New York. From that day on Maurice became Moshe to me. I think of him whenever I go to Sammy's Rumanian Jewish restaurant where the Parkway used to be. I recommend Sammy's highly, but suggest you make two reservations as I do — one for a table at the restaurant, and a second for a private room at Lenox Hill Hospital. That's really my soul food — the peppers with garlic, the breaded veal cutlet the size of a baseball mitt, the Rumanian tenderloin that hangs over the plate and the silver dollar potatoes. My stomach keeps repeating "Schmuck, schmuck . . ."

Although no one ever went to Las Vegas for food, in the old days there was one great Italian restaurant on the Strip — Louie's. I was taken there by Ben "Bugsy" Siegel when I worked for him at the Flamingo Hotel. Only the newspapers dared call him "Bugsy." Even his children called him "Mr. Siegel." He could have played George Raft in a movie. He was the epitome of style and sartorial splendor. But all he ever ate was spaghetti and meatballs.

I think I should go on record now by naming some of my favorite dishes at some of my favorite restaurants. I must start with my number one Paris restaurant, Chez L'Ami Louis. The foie gras, the roast chicken, the snails, the gigot made by that old man, Antoine Magnin, just can't get any better. And those incredible potatoes cooked with garlic and duck or chicken fat!

At the formal, restrained Taillevent I always have the seafood sausage and the duck with lemon. That place is pretty nouvelle but they're careful with me because they know I'm not a cuisine man.

Late at night in Paris, I like Brasserie Lipp, filled with local show-business personalities. I always have their great choucroute garni, sauerkraut with pork and sausages. Once I ordered the ris de veau, expecting rice with veal. Was I shocked to get sweetbreads!

That sort of thing keeps happening to me. Remember *cuatro services*? In Rome, I once confused the words fragole with fagioli so instead of strawberries for dessert, I got string beans. Usually things work out better for me in Rome. Try going to Cesarina with Alberto Sordi and have that terrific bollito misto with the green sauce, or some of the unusual pasta at Papa Giovanni with Raf Vallone.

And even now I can taste the ice cream tartufo I had at Tre Scalini with Vittorio Gassman. Just try! Ah, piacere de Roma.

I would never think of leaving Europe without a stop in London, where I must have the cassoulet and pheasant smitane at the Connaught and the creamy risotto at Harry's Bar. I also like the Dorchester Grill, smoked Scotch salmon at the Guinea Grill and, if it's the right season, the whitebait at Wheeler's.

My serious eating in New York begins at La Grenouille, one of the most beautiful and gracious restaurants I know. The original owner, Charles Masson, was a Soulé graduate, as were so many other of the city's top restaurateurs. Now his widow, Giselle, and their son, Charles, keep the place going beautifully. I like to start dinner with their baked lobster. It's for two as an appetizer, but I can never get Jeanette to share it with me, so what the hell, I eat it all. Then the thick loin veal chop with little potatoes and mushrooms, or their duck. And it's one place I always eat dessert — either the homemade sherbets or the harlequin soufflé, half chocolate, half vanilla or Grand Marnier.

Lutèce is like a lovely French country restaurant and the owner, André Soltner, is *the* master chef. He always comes to the table and asks what I feel like having. It's the only place where I say, "You decide." I've never been sorry.

For serious Italian food, I now go to Il Nido. With those mirrors and the etched glass, it's a beautiful place to be and I'm crazy about the ravioli malfatti — spinach and cheese without the pasta wrapping — the tortellini and the veal cutlet Milanese. That's not an easy dish to make correctly. But for a classic paillard of veal, I like the Four Seasons Grill at lunch.

I enjoy Le Cirque. Even though it's a little noisy and a little crowded for me, the food is excellent. And where else can I be greeted by a maître d' of the old school who has such flowery openers as "May the sun shine on your head until your hair turns to pure gold." I especially like Le Cirque after theater when Sirio Maccione himself grates the white truffles on top of the fettucine. That has to be the ultimate late night meal.

In Los Angeles, it's Morton's for the action, the lemon chicken and the apple cake, Spago for the beautiful people and Wolfgang Puck's pizzas, and Chasen's for memories. How can I forget the first time I went there was on a Sunday, and Carole Lombard and Clark Gable were in the first booth? Dave Chasen was a sweetheart and his wife, Maude, carries on his tradition. My favorite dishes there are not on the menu — the chili, the hobo steak roasted in salt and sliced at the table, and the beef braciole, a thick slice of rare prime rib with the bone, spiced, then quickly seared on a grill after it is carved.

Naturally, after all of these years of restaurant-going, I have developed a few traditions and quirks. The highest compliment I can receive is to have friends ask me to order for them. On a few occasions, I have goofed. When I appeared with Judy Garland at the Palace, she was going through a trying time and was very tense. I tried to amuse her and keep her relaxed by taking her out for an early dinner before the show.

She was a warm and generous person and she really loved to eat, but she was always nervous about her weight. I told her one night we'd go to Chinatown because the food is not fattening. "I hear they use alley cat instead of chicken," she said. She had obviously been talking to Jeanette. I ordered clams with black bean sauce, crisp whole fried flounder and a delicious stir-fried combination of chicken, lobster and all sorts of Chinese vegetables, which came out first. There was a big, black round thing on top. Judy asked what it was.

"That's a very rare and exotic Chinese mushroom," I told her. "It's such a delicacy they only use one to a portion, just as a French chef uses a slice of truffle."

As I was speaking, that exotic mushroom began to move, right off the plate, across the table and up the wall. Judy threw her head back and began to scream. Tears were rolling down her cheeks. I started to shake her, thinking she was hysterical. That didn't work, so I slapped her face. She stopped for a second, then hauled off and gave me a belt. "What the hell's the matter with you, you idiot? I'm not hysterical, I'm laughing." Since then, I've never ordered rare and exotic Chinese mushrooms.

I always respect a restaurant's dress code. If a man opens a restaurant, he has the right to decide how he wants his clientele to dress. A customer can decide if he wants to dress that way, and if not, he can go elsewhere. There are lots of choices. But it is important that a restaurateur should stick to his code, even for celebrities. The only exception, in my opinion, should be for someone like an Albert Einstein. I decided that after a near-disaster at "21." I was having a drink at the corner of the bar with Bess Myerson, and we were in view of the door. A man walked in, wearing thick-soled high shoes that were half-laced, crumpled cotton pants, a lumber jacket and a turtleneck sweater *with* a tie. He was covered with gray dust — not exactly the preferred dress code at "21." He looked around, a little bewildered, and in a second he was surrounded by ten assistant managers. Bess and I recognized him immediately and ran to his aid. We explained to the staff that he was Sir Jacob Epstein, the sculptor. He had just come from his studio and was being honored at a private dinner upstairs. As he walked to the elevator, I said to Sheldon Tannen, "What are you guys so upset about? After all, he *was* wearing a tie."

With all the time I spend at "21" it's no wonder that it's the setting for some of my favorite recollections. Once on Jeanette's birthday, we went to the opera to hear the great Richard Tucker sing, and he and his wife, Sara, invited us to a supper afterward at "21." They were our neighbors in Great Neck and were great company — Richard because he was an operatic eater and Sara because she was one of the best Jewish cooks I ever knew. After singing a tough role in an opera, Tucker liked nothing better than to go to "21," have two Jack Daniel's and a large supper.

When we were halfway through our meal, a group of Italians came in, among them Walter Chiari. He was long famous as a comedian but newly famous everywhere for his romance with Ava Gardner. We became good friends while doing a TV show in Rome. There was lots of hugging and kissing, Italian-style, and so no one listened very carefully to introductions. At the end of our meal there was a surprise. Sara had called and ordered a birthday cake for Jeanette. The waiters brought it over and gathered around the table singing "Happy Birthday." The Italians jumped up and came over to join in.

Inevitably, Richard Tucker's beautiful tenor took over even at half-voice. Listening for a second, Chiari turns to him and says, "You're not a bad singer. You've got a pretty good voice."

"Walter," I said. "Meet Richard Tucker."

They all did a double-take. "Bravo, Maestro! Bravo!" they yelled. Then they began, "Bis! Bis!"

And, consummate professional that he was, Richard Tucker stood up, bowed, and for the whole room complied with an encore of "Happy Birthday."

As far as I'm concerned, the greatest advantage in being well known is having the ability to get a good table and special attention at a restaurant.

When I get to a hotel where I'm going to be for more than two days, the first thing I do is send a bottle of scotch or brandy to the chef. Then I go down to see him and we talk about the menu for dinner. I do that in an airplane, too — I stick my head into the cockpit and say, "Hi, guys!" I like to get personal with the person in control.

Most of all, perhaps, it's important not to expect too much from a simple place in an out-of-the-way area. Once in a while, there may be a pleasant surprise, like at the superb French restaurant, Le Français, in the unlikely town of Wheeling, Illinois, but generally that is an exception.

I order simple things in simple places. It's the strategy that works for me every year during the U.S. Open when I want to eat close to the Tennis Center in Flushing. Every night for two weeks we go to Bacigalup's, an Italian restaurant on Main Street. I take a table for between eight and twelve people every night and I've worked out a series of dependable menus with the chef. But once in February, after going to an indoor tennis match in Flushing, I went looking for Bacigalup's. I swear to God, I drove all over Flushing and up and down Main Street maybe two dozen times. It was nowhere to be found. I told this to Peter Stone, who had been there with us many times.

"I just can't find the place!" I said.

"Alan," Peter said, "Bacigalup's only exists during the U.S. Open. It's the Italian *Brigadoon.*" I called the restaurant the next day to see if he was right. He wasn't.

Choosing the best of what you find locally applies to wines also. I was once in Nashville doing a TV special and I took my crew of sixteen out to dinner in the gourmet-gourmet room of the Hyatt-Regency. When I had given the dinner order, a most unusual sommelier arrived at the table. She was twenty-two and wearing a short, tiny skirt, black net stockings and had a Southern drawl you could cut with a knife. I glanced at the wine list and then, wanting to test her expertise, I said, "What would you recommend?"

Without a second's hesitation she pointed to a wine on the list — one I had never heard of, a vin du pays from Tennessee. "I think this one is real fine," she drawled. I asked her why she chose it, and she answered, "Because it's the only one we have enough of for a group this size." It may be the most intelligible thing any sommelier ever said to me.

LA GRENOUILLE'S CÔTE DE VEAU GRAND-MÈRE

FOR EACH SERVING

Prepare vegetable garnish first. Remove veal chop from refrigerator while doing so as it should be cooked at room temperature.

Place 1 teaspoon diced lard or blanched bacon in an 8-inch sauté pan or skillet and heat it. When it begins to melt and brown slightly, add 1 medium-size potato cut into ¾ inch dice or balls. Sauté over moderately high heat until potatoes are tender and just beginning to turn golden — about 8 minutes. Remove and reserve. Add 4 medium-size sliced mushroom caps, and sauté until golden brown and liquid has evaporated. Return potatoes to pan, season with salt and pepper and keep warm.

In a separate heavy-bottomed pan of about the same size, heat 1 tablespoon of unsalted butter until foam begins to subside. Sprinkle a 7- to 8-ounce loin veal chop with salt and pepper and sauté over moderate heat, allowing about 8 minutes for each side. When you turn the chop, add to the pan 2 branches of fresh thyme or ½ teaspoon dried thyme, 2 to 3 tarragon leaves, 1 chopped garlic clove and ½ bay leaf. Continue cooking chop with the herbs. When chop is done, remove from pan and keep warm.

Drain all fat and herbs from the pan. Add 1 table-spoon butter. Add one thinly sliced shallot, sauté for two minutes, then add 3 tablespoons dry white wine. Raise heat so wine reduces to a shiny glaze. Remove from heat and stir in a generous teaspoonful of un-salted butter, scraping in coagulated pan juices. Adjust seasonings.

Arrange veal chop on a plate, surround with pota-toes and mushrooms. Pour wine-butter sauce over all. Serve immediately. It is possible to do several chops at once in this manner. Just be sure they are sautéed in a pan that is large enough so they do not touch as they cook. Increase the potato and mushroom combination accordingly, but there, too, use a pan that will hold the vegetables in a single layer without crowding.

CHEZ L'AMI LOUIS'S ROASTED GARLIC POTATOES

SERVES 4 TO 6

Peel and quarter 6 large, old, boiling potatoes. Boil for two minutes in well-salted water. Drain and cool thoroughly.

Preheat oven to 400 degrees. Cover the bottom of a heavy baking pan with a thin film of rendered chicken fat and light vegetable oil. About 1 tablespoon of each should do. Place potatoes in pan in a single layer and add 6 large crushed garlic cloves.

Roast for about 45 minutes, or until potatoes are tender and golden brown. If garlic begins to turn dark brown, remove from pan and discard. Shake pan and turn potatoes several times during roasting. Add more fat or oil if pan seems dry.

When cooked, potatoes should be sprinkled with salt and pepper. Alan King usually makes these potatoes when he is roasting meat or chicken and bastes them with some of the pan juices from the roast.

CHAPTER ELEVEN

"Hi! My Name Is Kevin, I'm Your Waiter..."

Just as Moses handed down the Ten Com-mandments to his people, Alan King hands down these edicts he thinks will ensure good eating. As with most other things, he expresses his views on restaurants in a way that implies that anyone who differs is slightly crazy, or at least, incomprehensible. Although I agree with most of his don'ts, in a few instances I think he is the loser. Ethnic restaurants tend to be better in ethnic neighborhoods, for example, and besides the food, there is the enriching experience of an entirely different cul-ture. The food is usually less expensive under such cir-cumstances, also, the most obvious example being Chinese food in and out of Chinatown.

I have also found a lot of very good food and di-verting scenes in restaurants that have no tablecloths, although I do agree that paper placemats with games or menus printed on them generally herald disaster. And as for going to a restaurant I have never been to before, it's almost what I live for — the surprise, the challenge, the venture into the unknown. But, as already stated, the last thing Alan King wants when he goes out to dinner is a surprise, a valid if different point of view.

HINTS FOR FINDING GOOD RESTAU-rants are easy to come by. But equally important is knowing how to avoid the bad ones.

Avoid restaurants that have signs saying, "Come one, Come all. Fun for the entire family." It's sure to mean there'll be a grandmother carrying a screaming child around the dining room.

———•———

My father taught me there's no such thing as a free lunch. Resist places offering free hors d'oeuvres.

———•———

Resist offers to eat or drink all you want at a fixed price. If you don't get sick, you feel you haven't beaten the house.

———•———

Never mind the "Happy Hour." I don't want to be told I have to be happy between five and six, especially if I've had a bad day. When I want a miserable hour, no one can stop me from having it.

———•———

If you're unhappy with your married life, visit a singles bar and consider the alternative. It should drive you back to your spouse.

———•———

I never go to a salad bar with fake bacon bits and twenty kinds of dressings, each of which looks like an open can of moldy house paint.

———•—

The same goes for fix-your-own-dessert bars. The bar is always surrounded by rotten kids spraying each other with canned dairy whitener.

———•—

If there are no tablecloths, forget it.

———•—

Paper placemats with games or menus printed on them are no substitutes.

———•—

If a restaurant has a theme, I run the other way. Do you know what it's like to walk into The Buccaneer and be greeted with an "Ahoy, mates!" from someone wearing an eye-patch, a hook for an arm and a pegleg? I believe in hiring the handicapped, but this is ridiculous.

———•—

The same is true for Ye Olde Anything themes, where the waitresses dress like wenches and *F* stands for *s* on the menu. Faufagef taste just like faufagef.

———•—

If a waiter comes over and says, "Hi! My name is Kevin, I'm your waiter," I say, "Like hell you are," as I get up and leave.

———•—

I avoid all restaurants on the tops of the buildings except for the Terrace at Butler Hall in New York. Usually the better the view the worse the food. If it also revolves, I ask the waiter for "a double Dramamine, soda and a twist."

No music is the safest rule, whether it's live or piped in. And certainly no strolling guitars or accordions playing requests. I don't want to hear Guido singing "The Anniversary Waltz" in Yiddish . . . not when I'm eating.

"You gotta be really hungry to eat the food here," I say when opening my act in a nightclub that serves dinner. In all my years I've found only two exceptions — the old Versailles in New York and the old Copacabana for its Chinese food.

I wait at least six weeks before going to a restaurant that has had a favorable review. It's got to be a madhouse, the way Rao's was when Mimi Sheraton gave it three stars. They went so crazy trying to handle everyone, they finally tore the phone off the wall.

If a restaurant is empty, I don't want to disturb the silence, so I don't go in. Somebody must know something.

Stay away if there is a neon beer sign in the window.

I hate set menus. I like to set my own menus.

I hate menus that say "No substitutions. No half orders, and no sharing." I write on the menu "P.S. No tips."

I resent menus in the United States printed in any language other than English. I reject the notion that because I cannot read French or Italian, I know nothing about food.

I skip restaurants that require reservations a month in advance.

Ditto those that have fixed seatings. They want me there at six or nine, but I get hungry at seven-thirty.

Too much of the wrong kind of service stinks — compulsive water-pourers and ashtray cleaners, even if the ashtrays are not dirty. In California they pour coffee into the cup after every sip. I wait for it to cool and the waitress comes along with a boiling pot and screws it up.

I'm suspicious of places that have walls covered with autographed pictures of show-business "stars" I never heard of.

I hate listening to a waiter or captain recite off-menu specials. My neck gets stiff looking up, and I can never remember if the peas are with the chicken or the lamb and the morels with the veal or beef. And God forbid you should ask how much these items cost.

I hate menus with dozens of "specials" cards stapled around the edges. In trying to find what's on the regular menu, you always find yourself sneaking a look like a gambler picking up his hole card.

I never go to restaurants with a waterfall. I have a weak bladder.

I agree with Calvin Trillin about avoiding restaurants with names that are improbable descriptions, such as The Purple Goose, The Blue Kangaroo or The Quilted Orangutan.

I never go to restaurants named after days of the weeks or months — Monday, Tuesday, Wednesday . . . January, February, March . . . If I have to say to someone, "Should we meet Tuesday at Friday's? Or should it be Friday at Tuesday's?" I feel like I'm part of an Abbott and Costello routine.

Run for the door if there are paintings on velvet that glow in the dark.

Or paper flowers on the tables.

Or Chianti bottles with candles in them.

I never go to a restaurant that has a bulletin board in the lobby that says "Chamber of Commerce every Monday, Rotary every Tuesday."

If the coatroom attendant says you don't need a check, be prepared to wait an hour for your coat. If you have one of those plaid-lined Burberrys, do as I do: put a piece of salami in your pocket so you'll be able to identify it.

If I ask for a dish cooked in a certain way — say, the duck breast well done — and I'm told the chef won't cook it that way, I tell the chef what to do with it. Whose dinner is it, anyway?

I never try to use chopsticks. All through the Orient I carried my own fork and I rented it out to anyone who got tired of chopsticks — which took about three minutes.

I refuse to enter a restaurant in the required tie and jacket and have to take off my shoes. I never eat on the floor.

I never eat in an ethnic restaurant in an ethnic neighborhood, unless it's a Chinese restaurant in a Jewish neighborhood.

I never make reservations for an odd number of people, like three or five. They usually give you a table for two or four with an extra chair. Always make a reservation for an even number and after being seated, tell them the missing guest just got hit by a car.

A final tip. If you go to a restaurant with a crowded parking lot and do not want to wait an hour and a half to get your car back, do as I do. Wait for the people in your party to go into the restaurant. You stay behind and say to the parking attendant, "Someone in my party has a very serious heart condition. There is an oxygen emergency kit in the trunk of the car, so I hope you'll keep it handy." That way, the car will be right at the door when you need it.

CHAPTER TWELVE

Shot Glasses I Have Known

Although he has developed an appreciation of good wine and prides himself on a well-stocked cellar, Alan King still has an obvious admiration for the men who can hold their liquor — what he calls "the hard stuff." As he talked about the great drinkers, bars and bartenders he has known, there was repeatedly the sense of awe and respect he felt for the biggest belters. But only those with style. "Drinkers, not Drunks," he says.

It is perhaps the most dated of his notions and he is quick to admit that. It would not be accurate to say that they don't make drinkers the way they used to. They do, apparently, in ever-increasing numbers, but fortunately more now wind up as members of AA. Alan did insist on a responsible note in this chapter. "Great drinkers never drive," he said. "They have chauffeurs or take cabs. Often they cannot remember how they got home."

The reader, having come this far, deserves to be toasted, and in that, Alan joins me. We should toast

each other, and Jeanette, who may be the world's best
sport. To have gone into this collaboration as acquaint-
ances and to have come out as friends is no small tri-
umph, and we both drink to that.

A S YOU READ THESE PAGES, REMEMBER
this is not a medical report or a moral posi-
tion — just remembrances.

It seems fitting that this book, like so many of
my evenings, should end in a saloon. Drinking and
eating are parallel pleasures, but remember that
parallel, by definition, means they never meet.
When I eat, I eat. When I drink, I drink. To do both
at once might shock the system.

My rules of drinking are simple. Gin with ice,
soda and twist before dinner. No tonic, which is only
to be taken to ward off malaria. No lime because it's
too sweet. After dinner it's scotch on the rocks. Beer
is fine anytime. Brandy or cognac is too stimulating
and then the only way Jeanette can get me to sleep
is to hit me on the head with a baseball bat.

Great drinking should be done in great bars
and there is no formula for creating one. It's a combination of setting, customers, bartenders, memories and a touch of magic. A bar should feel like a
club — an intimate place where you can count on
meeting certain people so that you're never alone,
unless you want to be.

A great bartender knows when to talk and
when not to. Some of the best bartenders I knew

were those who understood just how and when to say, "Mr. King. . . . Don't you think you've had enough?"

A bartender who is a real pro will know by the third visit what a guy likes and just how he likes it. Recently I took my first trip to Bangkok and was impressed by the fantastic Oriental Hotel and its Bamboo Bar. Not only did the bartender know the gin-soda-twist formula by the second day, but I had the feeling I was drinking with the ghost of Joseph Conrad. Bars today have been taken over by Yuppies — grown men who ask for white wine with ice, or spritzers, or kirs, or drinks like Salty Dogs, Rusty Nails and something turquoise that looks like Windex. That's *almost* enough to drive me to abstinence.

Great bars do not have stools; I come to drink, not to rest. Good, fresh nuts and pretzels are the only permissible food. No waiters in short red jackets, offering meatballs or rumaki, are permitted, nor are table tents advertising stupid drinks in pineapples with little paper parasols stuck in them. And no Tiffany lampshades, fake or authentic. No plants. No suits of armor. No music, unless it's a piano player after ten.

My other requirements are that soda must come in bottles, not from a hose, and that ice should be in large, solid cubes. Shaved ice or hollow cubes melt and dilute the drink. Hard liquor should be served in double old-fashioned glasses, not stemware.

In Paris, I love the Bar Anglais downstairs in the Plaza Athenée. It's handsome, with mahogany paneling and Scotch plaid trim, and there are those delicious almonds that they serve. I also enjoy any pub in London.

During my Hemingway period, I hung around the bar of the Floridita in Havana and if I overdid the booze, I could sober up with that magnificent black bean soup.

I always have enjoyed the bar at the Pump Room in Chicago and love the small bar just off the street in the Algonquin. But the greatest bar in this country is at "21." The first time I walked into those bars I knew I was home.

I drink at the Polo Lounge at the Beverly Hills Hotel only because it has great bartenders and the best cocktail-lounge waiters I ever saw, which brings me to solving the Great Polo Lounge Gin Mystery. I had invested in the John McCunn Company, the importer of Tanqueray gin, and obviously started drinking it. The Polo Lounge then was one of the few places that had Tanqueray. I was making a film and every evening, when I got back to the hotel, I'd stop for a drink before going up to my room. I would order a Tanqueray with soda and a twist. Somehow it had a strange flavor I couldn't identify. I'd have the same drink late at night or for lunch and it was fine. Then back at the bar at six o'clock and it was off. I spoke to the bartender about it and we considered everything.

The next day, in the middle of the shoot, I had

an inspiration. As soon as I got to the bar, I asked the bartender to tell me exactly when he came on duty and how he prepared himself.

He said, "I get here at five-thirty, change my clothes, wash and shave."

"Do you use after-shave lotion?" I asked.

"And cologne," he answered indignantly.

"That's it," I said. "The mystery is solved." He splashed the after-shave on with his hands, and then he transferred the scent to every glass he touched. Bartenders, take note! I remained a loyal Tanqueray drinker until I switched my investment to Gordon's.

Restaurants with great bars don't have to serve great food, and the joint that proved the point was Toots Shor's. As a bar, it had everything and everyone, most especially sports people and newspapermen, none more eloquent or entertaining than Jimmy Cannon. But the food was a disaster. I would drink there every evening and then go someplace else for dinner.

One day Toots came over and said, "Hey, Crumb Bum. How come you drink here but you never eat?"

I said, "I do my eating at Pavillon and Henri Soulé has too much class to ask me why I never drink there."

Cannon said, "Why don't you make a deal?"

And I did. "I'll pay you twenty-five dollars a week for the privilege of not eating here," I said to Toots. And for the next five years, I gave him $100 a month. It was money well spent.

I drink for many reasons: I'm happy or I'm
worried; I'm nervous or I want to celebrate. Sometimes even because I'm thirsty. I drink for all of
those reasons put together during and after a
Broadway opening, especially if it's one of my plays.
Imagine how I felt when I was both the star
and co-producer of *The Impossible Years.* We
broke records in New Haven, Boston and Philadelphia, and by the time we got to New York we had
the largest advance sale of any straight play in
theater history, up to that time. Every theater
party bought tickets and two weeks before we
opened, the lines went halfway around the
block.

So of course we planned a huge opening night
party at the Americana Hotel — black tie, lavish
food, gallons of champagne — and we invited all the
backers, stars, press, the works. Then the review
came in from *The New York Times.* "Alan King is a
very funny man," it read. "Someone ought to write
a play for him." From there on the evening went
downhill, right into the toilet. For once, all the crit-
ics agreed — television, print, all of them. The play
was a bomb.

I walked out alone and proceeded to drink in
every bar I saw. The only thing that saved me was
New York's four A.M. closing law. At four-thirty I
wound up at the Market Diner on Eleventh Avenue,
starved. I had three scrambled eggs, crisp bacon,
toast, the kind of greasy home fries I remember
from my days on the road and two glasses of milk.
Then I stepped outside and joined the other bums

throwing up on the curb. I was the one in the tuxedo.

From there, I went to the Luxor Baths and by nine A.M. I was feeling almost human. Still dressed in black tie, fortunately with an overcoat, I had a couple of beers and went back to the theater. The lines were gone and by eleven o'clock we had sold only one ticket. But the silence outside was compensated for by the ringing of telephones inside. All of the theater parties wanted their money back.

We had a meeting with our ad agency to decide what to do. Some genius said, "We close." But I, gaining courage from my early morning libations, recalled the immortal word of my sainted Uncle Hymie. "Bullshit!" I said. "We fight!"

That night we went on and I could hear the reluctant shuffling of feet coming down the aisle. It cost between $50 and $150 for one of those theater-party tickets and the husbands didn't want to come anyway. With those reviews, the sound of feet walking in reminded me of convicts shuffling back to their cells. I took two straight shots of scotch.

The first scene when the curtain went up was me talking on the phone. Just at that moment, a fire engine answering a call gets stuck in traffic right outside the theater. The siren keeps whirring and screaming. I say to myself, "Alan, you're in trouble!" But thank God for all those years playing vaudeville, cheap saloons and burlesque. I wait for what seem like the longest minute and a half of my life. Then I scream into the phone: "You'll have to talk louder. There's a goddam fire in the neighbor-hood."

The whole audience broke into laughter and applause and the tension was over. They loved the play.

The next day we called all the theater-party committees and invited them to the show as our guests. "Then if you don't like it," we told them, "you can have your money back. But you must come to see it."

It ran with me in it for one year and three months, then another year without me. Later, MGM made it into a movie and David Niven played my role. Obviously he was the only one suave enough. It was a wonderful year, but an impossible night.

This may sound strange, but at times drink helped clear my mind. If I had been sober one night at La Rue's in Los Angeles, I might not have recovered something I lost. The great Lip, Leo Durocher, an old friend, was managing the Giants and had just won four straight from the Cleveland Indians in the World Series. He took the team to Tokyo for some exhibition games. Leo is a very generous guy and wanted to bring back special presents for friends. He bought some black-dyed vicuña — the first ever. Until then, vicuña only came in natural. He gave a topcoat's-worth of cloth to me, George Raft, Tony Martin and Harry Karl, a shoe tycoon who was then married to The Body, Marie McDonald. I went to my tailor, Emil Klein, to have the coat made.

Klein said to me, "Mr. King. I cannot take the

responsibility for this. I have never seen cloth so soft and so fragile. And besides, even with your cloth, it would cost five hundred dollars.''

"Emil, I don't care," I said. "The man brought it back for me and he has to see me wearing it. Make the coat.'' It was so special I couldn't find an occasion good enough for it and it stayed in the closet.

Three or four months later, I was going to Las Vegas and from there to Los Angeles. It was winter and I knew I'd see Leo, so I figured I'd take the coat. In those days, I gambled heavily and I always drank at the same time so I would have the courage to go on being an idiot. I lost all of my money and my credit ran out.

The word was out all over town. I continued drinking and carrying the coat over my arm as I made the rounds of casinos. As a last resort I walked into the Sands Hotel and there was the boss, Jack Entratter, who was my pal since the Copa days. "Jack, I've got to have some money to shoot crap," I pleaded.

"Tomorrow when you're sober," he answered.

I begged him, "Jack, I've got to get even!"

"You were even when you started, Putz. But all right, here's five hundred dollars and that's it," he said.

I drop the coat on a chair in the lounge and rush to the crap table. I put the whole five hundred on the line and up come the double sixes. I walk back to the lounge and the coat is gone. I tell Entratter, who laughs. "Just to show you what a losing streak you're on," he says, "someone went south with your coat." I was miserable.

I went on to California and the first night there I was invited to a party given by Harry Karl at La Rue's, which was a wonderful restaurant. I was telling Tony Martin about my coat as we were sitting at the bar having a drink, waiting for Cyd Charisse to join us. I look up and see a man walk in with a woman. "You're not going to believe this, Tony, but that guy is wearing my coat," I say.

"You're crazy," Martin says. "Just keep drinking and don't make any trouble."

"I swear, Tony. It's mine. It's an Emil Klein cut," I say.

"Don't embarrass me and don't make a scene," Tony says. "And don't embarrass Harry."

All during dinner, I watch the door so I can see when this guy leaves. Just as we're close to dessert, I see him at the checkroom. I get up and Tony realizes where I'm going and he grabs me. I push his hand away and walk over to the door.

"Excuse me, sir," I say, trying to be calm and polite. "Excuse me, but that's a very lovely coat."

"Oh, thank you very much," he says.

"I never saw a black-dyed vicuña before," I say.

"Oh, is that what it is?" he answers. "I thought it was cashmere. It's warm."

"It's vicuña and it's hot," I tell him. "And it also happens to be mine." I realize that he is not the one who stole it, only the one who bought it.

"Are you crazy, or just drunk, young man?" he says.

"Look, sir," I say, "I don't want to make a scene but I'm not above it. Bear with me for a moment. Custom tailors, as you probably know, always stitch a small label with the customer's name and date of purchase in the inside pocket. Please reach into that pocket and tell me what you find."

He turns the pocket inside out and there's the label: Alan King.

He just peels off the coat, hands it to me and walks out into the cold night, without saying a word. The guy had class.

I put the coat on and walk back to the table. All I hear is Tony Martin saying, "I'll be a son of a bitch. It *was* his coat." When I got back home after the trip, I put the coat in the closet. A week later, my houseman quit and, not satisfied with his severance, he too went south with my coat. The only time I ever wore it was on the trip from the checkroom to the table.

Half of my drinking time is spent waiting for Jeanette to get dressed. One night in Acapulco we were going to a big fancy party and when she went up to dress, I knew I had time for a few drinks. I sat down at the bar and ordered a tequila. That, I could pronounce. A few weeks before, I had been debating the reasons for the Vietnam War on the Dick Cavett show. I said that it was the shoot-from-the-hip, macho, John Wayne hero image that led us into it. I had never met Wayne.

All of a sudden that night at the bar, a hand the size of a ham hock grips my shoulder and there, looming over me, is a granite face like you see carved on Mount Rushmore. It was Big Duke himself. I think to myself, "Here's where I really get it. He's going to have me for an hors d'oeuvre." As my shoulder grows numb, he drawls, "I hear you had quite a lot to say about me on TV." For once, I can't even ad-lib a belch.

"Ya know," he continues, "we gotta lot of mutual friends and I checked you out. They tell me you've got a big mouth but you're not a bad guy . . . for a pinko."

"I checked you out with the same mutual friends, and they said you were kind, considerate, noble and would never beat up on an old, fat, frightened Jew," I answer.

He starts to smile. "Well, why don't we discuss our mutual friends over a couple of drinks?" he says.

After about two dozen tequilas, we were on our way to a lasting friendship. At ten-fifteen I'm called to the phone. It's Jeanette. "Where the hell are you?" she says. "Don't you know you're supposed to be dressed by ten?"

"Relax, Pilgrim," I drawl. "I'm having a drink with John Wayne."

"Swell," she says, "and I'm in bed with Paul Newman."

"Well, as long as we're both having a good time . . ." I say, and I hang up.

Not all of my drinking expeditions have been that dramatic. One of the mildest and pleasantest took place at La Bonne Auberge in Antibes. Jeanette and I were with a few friends and as we walked to our table, I noticed Bess and Harry Truman having dinner with a small group. He was no longer president and was on vacation. We had met at many Democratic functions, but I didn't want to interrupt his dinner. But he recognized me and asked me over.

After being introduced to Bess and the other friends, I inquired as to how the Truman Library was coming, and wondered if there was anything I could do, like fund-raising.

He said, "I'm glad you asked me that. Can we discuss this in private for a few minutes?" And so we walked out to the cocktail lounge.

He nods to the bartender, who immediately pours two bourbons. Truman winks at me and says, "I'm not supposed to drink and Mother watches me like a hawk." He then ordered another round. I'm not a bourbon drinker, but I couldn't let my favorite president drink alone.

One of my childhood idols was the incomparable John Barrymore. Nobody could drink like he could — and with such style. He gave one of his greatest performances at Leon and Eddie's on a Sunday. That was celebrity night and things began to get lively at midnight. They were honoring Martha Raye, and the place was packed with stars like Milton Berle, Joe E. Brown, Gertrude Niesen,

Mike Todd, Billy Rose and Eleanor Holm and the Ritz Brothers.

At two A.M. in walks Barrymore, held up by his loyal disciples, Victor Jory and John Carradine. It's the only time I ever saw a drunk being carried *into* a place.

Barrymore goes to the back of the room and sprawls facedown on the table. Eddie Davis, the emcee and owner of the club, introduces the stars and they each do a turn. I'm praying he doesn't call Barrymore. It would be too embarrassing.

Suddenly I hear, "Ladies and gentlemen. This is an easy introduction. The world's greatest actor, John Barrymore."

There's a standing ovation and I'm looking for a place to hide. Barrymore gets up and he's weaving so much that the spotlight can't focus on him. But the closer he gets to the stage, the straighter he becomes and by the time he's in front of the mike, he's erect, like a drooping flower that suddenly gets the water it needs. There's a hush in the room and then the voice that made Hamlet famous begins: "Ladies and gentlemen. It's been many years since I have been to Leon and Eddie's. The last time I was here, I was drinking." A small, nervous laugh ripples through the audience.

"As I walked down Fifty-second Street, the pavement became a path in the Garden of Eden. The canopies of the clubs on both sides of the street looked like the tents of Araby and as I entered Leon and Eddie's, the portals became the Pearly Gates."

All you could hear was the ice tinkling in the glasses.

"Louis Katz, the maître d', was Aladdin and as he rubbed his magic lantern, this saloon turned into the Taj Mahal. And as I stood on this stage and looked out at the faces, the men were Romeos and all the women, Juliets.

"But as I said, *that* night I was drinking. As I stand here now, sober, may I say you are the ugliest bunch of bastards I have ever seen." And with that, he flashed the famous profile, strode off the stage, marched back to his table and, as he sat down, missed the chair and fell flat on his ass.

The room exploded with screams, cheers and laughter.

Saving my best memories for last brings me to the one and only Joe E. Lewis, undoubtedly the single most monumental drinker. He made Dean Martin look like the Reverend Jerry Falwell. He was also the kindest and most generous man I ever knew. I owe everything to Joe E. Lewis. He taught me the really important things in life — drinking, gambling and throwing money away.

The New York nightclub season began officially when Joe E. Lewis opened at the Copacabana in September. The other clubs he played regularly were Ciro's in Los Angeles, the Beachcomber in Miami, the Chez Paree in Chicago and the Roosevelt Hotel in New Orleans. Those rooms belonged to Joe E. He could drink the labels off the bottles and during performances he kept shot glasses of scotch

at every ringside table, so that he could have a drink
as he moved around. Each time he'd lift a glass, Joe
E. would announce, "It is now post time . . ." and
the trumpet in the orchestra would sound the appro-
priate call.

Whenever someone asks me if I want water
with my scotch, I give them Joe E.'s answer: "I'm
thirsty. I'm not dirty." When his doctors told him to
stop drinking, he said, "I know more old drunks
than I do old doctors." But that night during his act
he announced, "I'm not drinking anymore. . . . I'm
not drinking any less, either."

I followed Joe E. around like a puppy. He was
my hero and my friend, almost a second father. I
even went with him to Hot Springs when he had to
dry out. By the time he got out of the pool, the water
was 100 proof.

"Booze for all," was one of his favorite lines and
he shouted it one night as we walked into a real
bust-out joint on Bourbon Street in New Orleans.
The B-girls flocked around us and ordered champagne. Joe E. drank scotch. I accidentally picked up
one of the girls' drinks and sipped it. It was ginger
ale, not champagne. I was outraged. I pulled Joe E.
aside. "Do you know what they're doing to you? Do
you know you're paying for champagne and they're
drinking ginger ale?"

"It's all right," he said. "In the interest of science, I'm performing an experiment. I want to see if
these broads drink as much ginger ale as I can drink
scotch."

They couldn't. By seven in the morning the girls were wiped out and Joe E. was still going strong.

His life and wit were captured in a book and then a movie, *The Joker Is Wild*. He really was. He never lost his sense of humor, not even when he was dead drunk and had used up all of his money and his credit, as he did one night in Las Vegas. "C'mon, Joe E." I said. "Let's get some sleep. You're broke." As I tried to lead him out of the room, he pushed me aside, elbowed his way to the crap table and climbed up on it. He laid his body across the table and placed his bet: "My life on the hard four!"

When he was stricken in Los Angeles, Sinatra rushed him to the emergency room of the Cedars of Lebanon Hospital. The doctor examined him and it didn't look good.

"What's the diagnosis?" he asked. "And don't lie to me."

"It doesn't look too bad," Frank lied. "They say you have a fifty-fifty chance."

Joe E. cracked that famous smile of his and quipped, "Take me to another hospital. I want better odds."

I was privileged to deliver the first eulogy at his funeral. I looked down at the coffin and said, "Before we begin, let's open a bottle of Johnny Walker Black and announce that it is now post time. Then if Joe E. doesn't get up, the services will proceed."

Is Salami and Eggs Better Than Sex?

Anyone who poses a question as provocative as this one should provide an answer. If you've read all the way through this book and are not just browsing in a bookstore, you're entitled to an answer.

Most of life's great pleasures satisfy the senses and the soul, as do food and sex, and with both, love is an essential ingredient. I have been lucky in both, having had the joy of good food and the love of my wonderful wife, Jeanette, almost all my life.

But are you mad? Of course salami and eggs is not better than sex. But why choose between them? For the ultimate pleasure, try following sex with salami and eggs — and don't forget the ketchup on the eggs and the cream cheese on the toasted bialy.

INDEX OF RECIPES